PEACEMAKING

Nine Lessons for Changing Yourself, Your Relationships, & the World

by Dr. Barbara Condron

If you desire to learn more about the research and
teachings in this book, write to School of Metaphysics
World Headquarters, Windyville, Missouri 65783.
Or call us at 417-345-8411.
Visit us on the Internet at www.som.org and www.peacedome.org

P
E
A
C
E

What is friendship?
Matthew Marian

A true friend is someone who aids you in your soul growth.
This means celebrating that part of each other that is
amazing, beautiful, connected, powerful,
really celebrating each other.

A friendship is lifting each other up striving for the good and
highest thoughts and experiences individually and collectively.

Friendship is listening, talking, sharing,
accepting, appreciating.
Friendship is separating people from their
thoughts and loving the person.

The Change...

"Dr. Barbara!" Jen Childers' voice said into the phone, "I didn't turn in my friendship paper." Her voice was somewhere between angst and remorse. She was talking about what she had written during our PeaceMakers gathering the week before.

A bit of background will be helpful to you here. PeaceMakers is what we call our Sunday morning meeting on the College of Metaphysics campus. The gathering is open to anyone who wants to share in spiritual communion. PeaceMakers began six summers ago in the backyard of the Dream Valley house when the kids from our annual Camp Niangua wanted a reason to see each other again. Since then it has grown and matured through many expressions. Sometimes we sing songs or compose them. Sometimes we do improvisational acting of stories from around the world. Sometimes the college thespians prepare a play they have created with PeaceMakers in mind. Sometimes we talk about our thoughts and feelings, take self-exam quizzes that often make us laugh at ourselves more than each other, and always we begin with a prayer for enlightenment around the world and end with a Circle of Love.

The PeaceMakers Jen was talking about was held in the upper chamber of the Peace Dome, an amazing white-domed room sixty feet in diameter that moves energy in incredible ways. A whisper on one side is heard equally around the room. I have come to think of this space as a place of no secrets.

This PeaceMakers was the close of a weekend unlike any other. Seventy-five people from across the Midwest had taken off work, some traveling for 10 hours, all to volunteer their time and effort toward preparing to host the world for the October 11th dedication of the world's first Peace Dome being built here on the campus of the College of Metaphysics. About sixty of us gathered making a large circle in the Dome. After the prayer and singing of "Peace in the Garden", a song the new college students had written in the first week of living here, I asked everyone to write their answer to "What is Friendship?"

After a respectable time I asked them to distill their ideas into one sentence, the cream of their thought.

Next came the fun and the insight. We numbered off in twos. The number ones formed an inner circle by standing shoulder-to-shoulder facing outward. Then the number twos came forward to face one of the people in the inner circle, thus forming an outer circle.

Once everyone had a partner the movement began. Those in the inner circle gave. They gave their thought of what friendship is to the person standing in front of them. The receiver was still, drinking in what was said. Everyone in the inner circle spoke simultaneously, so the attention had to be directed by both giver and receiver or the physical sound would easily overpower your experience. When silence was again experienced, the inner circle would move clockwise, the outer circle counterclockwise, until new partnerships were formed. The inner circle then gave to the outer circle. I call this experience the Spiritual Chakra because it functions as an energy transformer within and between and among people.

Once the inner circle had given to all of those in the outer circle, we traded places. The givers now became receivers, and the receivers became givers. Changes were happening moment to moment through it all. I asked people to write their thoughts, about their experience of giving and their experience of receiving. They turned in their papers and since friendship is an expression of love (which is a foundation for peace) you will find the thoughts from this day peppered throughout this book.

Jen was one of the people present during this PeaceMakers. Jen is a beautiful, bright 24-year-old from Dallas, Texas. Through her desire to share with others, we worked together to create a book of poems by two dozen spiritual teachers called <u>Kundalini Poetry</u>. The experience was rich for us, the divinely inspired poets, and for the reader. Over and over people have told us that their own Kundalini is stimulated when they read these poems.

We had been talking about this book in this phone conversation, and before Jen said goodbye she made her confession.

I was curious about why she hadn't turned in her paper. "How come?" I asked simply.

"It was a poem, and I thought it was silly."

I smiled. Jen like so many is prone to seeing her gifts as unworthy.
"Would you like to hear it?" she asked tentatively.
"Of course."

> "My heart goes grows pouring love
> Continuous love
> Devotion to loving
> Laughing with lips
> Connections revisited one by one
> Passion, intellect, security, fun
> Remaining open to give and receive
> love
> love
> love!"

"I just wanted to share that." Jen's sensitivity is keen, and so she is often miserly in giving herself opportunities to completely express simple truths.

"It's beautiful, Jen. Maybe next time you'll be freer to share it with the world." Then I thought again. "Jen you are such a pure soul. You need to give from your soul. We've all been taught to be ashamed of love. We have to change that in ourselves so we can help others change it. Give what you have, be who you are. It's quite beautiful."

Then I said, "You have given me the forward for the PeaceMaking book."

"I have?" Jen was incredulous.

"Absolutely. Can I put your poem in it?"

She said yes, and here it is.

Friendship. Remaining open. Laughing, loving, helping one another. These are the ways we make peace.

–Dr. Barbara Condron
The Peace Dome on the campus of the College of Metaphysics
Windyville, Missouri, United States of America, Planet Earth, Milky Way
Galaxy

M
A
K
I
N
G

...is in Us

Growing up I never seemed to have too many "friends" in my life. I felt like an outsider always looking in.

That is why I had to chuckle when Dr. Barbara Condron asked us to write about "What is Friendship?" that morning in the Peace Dome. I never considered myself as having too many friends. The facts were (so I thought) I had very few friends, if any. Oh sure, I had associations, acquaintances, but they seemed so disconnected, so distant.

I began to look around the circle of people, seeking some guidance as to the answer to the question. That is when I saw John Mestyanek. John is my classmate and I have always looked up to him. He has that "big brother" attitude written all over him. He looked up at me and gave me a warm and loving big smile, as he frequently does. I can count on him for that. Those times when I tend to feel lonely or downtrodden he is there with his big smile.

That is when the thought came to me – "Friendship is the love given in a smile."

We then formed into two groups, the givers formed the inner circle as the receivers formed the outer. As each person shared their thought of friendship, I received their thought. My entire body felt nervously tingly. I felt each person's love and affection. I wanted to breathe in each person. I could literally feel my heart opening.

I felt as if I could no longer hide behind my own limitations of feeling alone, unwanted or unworthy. With each new person, I felt my walls tumbling down as I awakened to the fact that we are never alone. We all desire to belong, be connected, accepted and loved by others. I began to fill so full that I felt I was about to burst. The energy continued to build inside me and throughout me. I felt so alive, rejuvenated as if I just walked out of a long, hot shower.

I was vibrating as I sat down to write about my experience. I do not believe I ever allowed myself to soak in so much love at one time. I started to look at friendship in a whole new light this morning. It is just as important to receive as it is to give. That was a new thought for me. I had until today believed as I had been told growing up that "it is always better to given than to receive." In this moment in the Peace Dome, surrounded by dozens of friends some I had met for the first time two days ago, I saw how much I blocked out or pushed others away because of my fears, my hurts and unwillingness to unconditionally receive. Equally I would hold back what I had to give for fear of rejection or possibly becoming hurt.

Now we switched places. Those who were in the inner circle moved to the outer and those of us on the outer, receiving circle moved toward the inner giving circle. As I looked each of the people in the eye and said what friendship is, each person smiled. It was a very natural response. I thought about how simple that is.

As I continued around the circle I felt more and more the love that permeated the entire room. I knew in that moment that I was loved.

As I write down these thoughts, I can see that friendship – divine friendship – can happen anywhere, any time, and any place, and it is shown through something as simple as a smile. This moment will always stay with me for it opened my heart to a whole world of friends.

Laurie J. Biswell
College of Metaphysics
August 3, 2003

P
E
A
C
E

Front cover photos (clockwise from top): One of the two dozen doves set free at the dedication of the Peace Dome on October 11, 2003. The Healing Wall at the Peace Dome. The Reflecting Pool on the grounds of the College of Metaphysics campus. Ceremonies in The Gambia synchronized with Peace Dome ceremonies in the U.S. The Great Room at COM. The Peace Dome on October 10th in the afternoon and the evening (next picture). In the second floor chamber of the Peace Dome. Friends at the South Pole participate in One Voice, the synchronized global reading of the *Universal Peace Covenant*. Below right, first floor of the Peace Dome.

Back cover: The Peace Dome on dedication day. College thespians who bring the Nobel Peace Prize Laureates to life touch the continents at the Healing Wall with Camp Niangua participant Logan Goldstein.

Photographers: Paul Madar, Emeka Onyekwere, Ernie Padilla, Daniel Condron, Lynn Arnold, and Barbara Condron.

The Contents

P
E
A
C
E

Lesson One

SMILE

"Let us always meet each other with a smile, for the smile is the beginning of love..."

WHAT IS FRIENDSHIP?
Stacy Ann Ferguson

Love. Concern. Connectedness. **Delight in another**.
Compassion. Active Self Respect. Honesty. Choice.
Experiencing Self with another.
Choosing to love, nurture and delight in another person.

Continuously choosing to be connected to, love, nurture and delight in another person.

Receiving
"Friendship is love with adventure"
"Friendship is the love that is given in a smile" Many perspectives

Giving: smiled so much my face hurt.
"Friendship is delight in another."   I delighted in each person.
Both: a little uncomfortable just being with people.

FRIENDSHIP IS LIKE A CAR RIDE
SHAWN SMITH

Its foundation / pavement is the light connectedness that we all
share with each other universally. Its vehicle for motion is love.
Its journey is giving & receiving with eye fixed toward mutual
self-awareness & soul growth. Its destination is compassion & understanding.
Friendship is a car ride whose pavement is connectedness; whose vehicle for
motion is love; whose journey is giving & receiving; and whose destination is compassion.

Friendship is connectedness, love, giving & receiving, & compassion.

Receiving — feeling of purity, truth & worthiness

Giving — deep sense of connectedness & experiencing
the light within feeling or peaceful knowing.

Each Sunday morning, most people in the College of Metaphysics community gather for what we call PeaceMakers. PeaceMakers have been meeting for five years now. Attending our evolution has been a source of delight for me and a privilege.

This meeting is the first of its kind in a new year – 2003; the year that will build toward the dedication of the world's first Peace Dome set for October 11th. Preparing our consciousness is the essential core of the message we want to convey when we welcome people from around the world to this place on Earth. We want to know peace, with our reasoning minds and our intuitive minds so we can be living examples of peace.

Since the School of Metaphysics was founded in 1973, thousands have learned the principles and practices that produce peace of mind. We have learned that to directly grasp the truth of peace means holding it in your mind and heart, expressing its beauty, its form, its spirit, and to be capable of teaching others to do the same. We want to embody the thoughts expressed so eloquently in the *Universal Peace Covenant*[1] thus bringing it to life for ourselves and for others.

Today begins this preparation.

The words "led by grace" come to mind as I describe what transpired this morning. I had been contemplating for days what direction we might move in. Of all the possibilities, my mind kept coming back to three: creating a musical-drama centered on well-known songs of peace arranged to tell the story of every person's quest, evolving the *Power of Prayer around the World Cantata* presented during the 1993 Parliament of the World's Religions, or experiencing a Circle of Love gathering which begins with a *Prayer for Enlightenment*[2], includes reciting the *Covenant* and concludes with a Circle of Love where all present join hands in a guided imagery of universal brotherhood and love.

The first two ideas were too early in their formative stages to share. They had yet to take a form that I could easily communicate. It would have been like a screenwriter working out his ideas with the director and actors before he even knows what they are. The result would fall somewhere between an improvisation and a collaboration, neither of which were compatible with how I knew PeaceMakers needed to evolve. This conclusion meant the more reasonable choice for tomorrow's PeaceMakers would be the Circle of Love. I went to sleep knowing this much and turned the matter over to my subconscious mind for clarification.

In the morning, PeaceMakers filled my mind. The gathering we call a Circle of Love begins with a Prayer for Enlightenment around the world, affirming the prevailing of peace on earth, and ends with the sharing of love among all in attendance and with the world and beyond which School of Metaphysics people have, for the past three decades, called a Circle of Love. The inner content of the gathering is variable.

I knew I wanted to include the *Universal Peace Covenant*. We had all made a commitment to read the *Covenant* once a day, and many of us wanted to commit it to memory, so we might know it by heart. I knew reading it this morning could be helpful especially if we took time to talk about what the words mean to us.

My conscious mind would have let it go at that. My inner, subconscious mind tugged at me. I had a strong sense that something was incomplete, unfinished.

Scanning my bookshelves in the hope that this sense would take on a physically recognizable presence, my eyes rested on a tiny book half an inch thick and about three inches by five inches. I reached for <u>The Words of Peace</u>.[3] Its diminutive size belies its expansive contents. Here are wisdom words from many of the Nobel Peace Prize laureates, some of the greatest people who ever breathed on this planet.

Opening the pages near the middle I found the words of a woman I had grown to admire – Mother Teresa, a Catholic nun who served in the streets of Calcutta and through her dedication to God and humanity founded over 100 missions around the world. Reading her thoughts, my conscious mind knew why I was experiencing the inner unrest. Here was the lesson for today's PeaceMakers.

We gathered in the College chapel, sitting on the floor in a circle. Before offering our prayer I shared my vision of daily gatherings once the Peace Dome is open. Each day whoever desires will come together to offer the *Prayer for Enlightenment* and read the *Universal Peace Covenant*. It will be like a breath of fresh air fortifying the thoughtform of peace every twenty-four hours. Whether spoken by one or by a thousand, the beauty of the still and open mind, entrained in unity, dedicated in connectedness, will have a profound effect upon all of us.

"Today," I said, "we begin preparing for this." We then offered in unison the *Prayer for Enlightenment*.

May Peace Prevail on Earth!

We pray for light in the people of North America
May enlightenment be in North America
May light be with us all ways.
May peace prevail on Earth.

We pray for light in the people of South America
May enlightenment be in South America
May light be with us all ways.
May peace prevail on Earth.

We pray for light in the people of Europe
May enlightenment be in Europe
May light be with us all ways.
May peace prevail on Earth.

We pray for light in the people of Africa
May enlightenment be in Africa
May light be with us all ways.
May peace prevail on Earth.

We pray for light in the people of Asia
May enlightenment be in Asia
May light be with us all ways.
May peace prevail on Earth.

We pray for light in the people of Australia
May enlightenment be in Australia
May light be with us all ways.
May peace prevail on Earth.

We pray for light in the people of Antarctica
May enlightenment be in Antarctica
May light be with us all ways.
May peace prevail on Earth.

We pray for light in the people of the Earth
May enlightenment be in Earth
May light be with us all ways
so that peace may prevail on Earth.

Amen.

I asked those present what they saw in their mind's eye when they spoke these words. Mari Hamersley and Erika Scholz spoke of the light spreading throughout the continents, blanketing the entire globe. While they spoke I saw my own thought echoed back to me, as this was often the image I created, and in that moment a new image was given to me. In it I saw the Earth herself radiating, glowing, from the inside out. The finer stuff of my mind was now active in a way I had been wanting.

Paul Blosser and Christine Madar talked about Pran, their native guide during the 1999 People to People sojourn to India, and others they know who live on six continents. Christine said she didn't know anyone who lives in Antarctica but she always thinks of penguins when the prayer moves to the South Pole. We all laughed, nodding in agreement. I too begin each continental mind visit where people I have physically met now live. For me, this is the focal point from which light emanates. It is the human element in my prayer, for I know this infusion of light and love helps keep those I love safe and secure.

It was Paul Madar's idea which gave me a new perspective of the prayer. He said he projects himself to the continent he is imaging, and once there radiates love and light throughout the continent. "What a concept!" I thought. The idea had never occurred to me, and I could appreciate it for its pure and honest maleness; its willingness to give. I knew I would think about this again and again in the coming days, opening my mind to its possibilities.

These experiences served as an appropriate introduction to the excerpts we would consider this morning. I spoke of the ideals in the *Universal Peace Covenant*. Its boldness in defining what makes peace. Literature worldwide is filled with ideas that try to talk about the concept by describing what it is not. Too often peace is defined as the absence of war, conflict, or disagreement. What a difference it will make when words like tranquility, calm, ease, security, and accord tumble from our minds as readily!

Our venture today, and probably for several future PeaceMakers, would be exploring the thoughts of those we have collectively honored and celebrated for their peace-making effort and skill. I began by reading the forward to the book, written by President Jimmy Carter several years before the peace prize was bestowed upon him. His thoughts are rich.

"In our private and individual lives, all of us have a need to seek for heroes. In our own personal ambitions and life – analysis of what opportunities present themselves to us, the talents that we have, the unpredictable future – we need those on whom we can depend as a pattern. How can we live an exemplary existence? The measurement of that, the pattern for it, the guide for our own lives, comes from our heroes. How can we justify our dreams? How can we confirm our beliefs? How can we prove to ourselves that what we have been taught as children is true? How can we alleviate our doubts? How can we, in our own often naturally dormant lives, be inspired to action, sometimes even at the sacrifice of our own immediate well-being? We derive those inspirations from heroes."[4]

These words, from a 1986 speech, open the mind and heart to the ideal of every human being. President Carter calls the people quoted in this book heroes of peace.

Wealthy Swedish industrialist and inventor, Alfred Nobel specified in his will that this prize was to be given for the organizing of peace congresses and efforts of disarmament, and for work for "fraternity between nations." The list of previous winners include political leaders like Theodore Roosevelt (1906) and Oscar Arias Sanchez (1987), humanitarians like Fridtjof Nansen of the Office of the United Nations High Commissioner for Refugees, Albert Schweitzer and Mother Teresa, Religious leaders like Archbishop Soderblom and the Dalai Lama of Tibet, scientists like Lord Boyd-Orr and Norman Borlaug whose work brought more food to a hungry world, and to practitioners of nonviolence such as the Quakers and the Peace People of Northern Ireland. The list goes on, stimulating the mind to open to the depth and breadth of what peace is and what it motivates human beings to do.

In her speech accepting the Nobel Peace Prize in 1979, Mother Teresa speaks to you, the individual. Her words touch the inner Self, opening the heart to what peace causes us to become. Her words ask us to reveal our Christ Self. Her honesty in self revelation is admirable.

"The poor are very wonderful people. One evening we went out and we picked up four people from the street. One of them was in a most terrible condition – and I told the sisters: you take care of the other three, I take

care of this one who looked worse. So I did for her all that my love can do. I put her in bed, and there was such a beautiful smile on her face. She took hold of my hand as she said just the words 'Thank you,' and she died."⁵

Mother Teresa spoke of the poor without derision or condescension, saying they are *"very wonderful people."* Her attitude echoed that of another great peacemaker whose efforts in peaceful noncooperation led him to be known as the Father of India – Mohandas K. Gandhi. It was Gandhi who first broke down the barriers of the caste system by lifting the untouchables by calling them Harijans meaning "children of God." A kindred soul, Mother Teresa continued this work for decades after Gandhi's assassination in 1948.

Mother Teresa often told the story of a sickly woman she brought in from the streets and cared for. All she could offer was a warm bed and her love. Mother Teresa described the beautiful smile on the woman's face.

"She took hold my hand as she said just the words 'Thank you,' and she died."

The beauty of Mother Teresa's character was in her work, her service, her daily expressions of love that make us stop and think twice about our own daily thoughts. How often do we build our experiences out of proportion? Headaches from traffic jams, hurt feelings from partially heard conversations, or people who are a pain in the neck take on a new perspective in light of how we live, how we die, and how we help each other. Mother Teresa's life demanded that we look at ourselves.

She knew this, not because she was a saint but because she was willing to face herself. This is clearly described in her acceptance speech:

"I could not help but examine my conscience before her, and I asked what would I say if I was in her place. And my answer was very simple. I would have tried to draw a little attention to myself, I would have said I am hungry, that I am dying, I am cold, I am in pain, or something, but she gave me much more – she gave me her grateful love. And she died with a smile on her face. As did the man whom we picked up from the drain, half eaten with worms, and we brought him to the home. 'I have lived like an animal

in the street, but I am going to die like an angel, loved and cared for.' And it was so wonderful to see the greatness of that man who could speak like that, who could die like that without blaming anybody, without cursing anybody, without comparing anything. Like an angel–this is the greatness of our people. And this is why we believe what Jesus had said: I was hungry–I was naked–I was homeless–I was unwanted, unloved, uncared for– and you did it to me."[6]

Mother Teresa learned from the experiences in her life and in so doing found the key to turning blame into appreciation. Through countless experiences with those who were alone and forgotten, in need of care, she found her own humanity.

I remember an article I read about Mother Teresa following her death in 1997. The reporter told the story of how he had gone to Calcutta in hopes of interviewing this amazing woman, finding out who she was, what made her do what she did. Upon arriving, he very quickly learned his answers in ways he never anticipated. Rather than stop what she was doing to have a mannerly chat, Mother Teresa thrust a babe into the reporter's arms telling him that if he were going to talk with her he would be coming with her, and he would be helping!

I saw the importance of "doing with" in that story. For years, being in the habit of social custom and my early politeness training, I was bound by propriety to stop whatever I was doing in deference to people like this reporter. All under the guise of human kindness. How many times had I burned a meal, forgotten a phone call, or kept others waiting because I had a lesson to learn about when to say "no," or "wait," or "later"?

Mother Teresa helped me realize the unkindness I allowed when distracted from the work of aiding those in need. Since my highest ambition is teaching teachers, what better way than to involve the able-minded and able-bodied in the experience of work that can heal an individual – or a planet?

Mother Teresa helped me understand that what I had believed was being rude was wrong-thinking. She set the example of how to think and act in a new way which I continue to teach myself every day.

Another reporter told of his experience which was a window into the intent of this frail-looking lady who owned only two sets of clothing, a rosary, and a Bible. After spending several days in the filth, disease, and poverty that surrounded Mother Teresa, the man's intellectual resolve was wavering. He began to wonder how she could spend day after day, through her own volition, in such a place that was not her homeland, far from her family, with little recompense of any kind.

After watching a baby die in her arms, the reporter found the courage to ask her, "How can you continue this work?"

Her answer was simple, "*I do it for Christ. I see my Christ in the eyes of each one. I do it for him.*"

To know such a pure and simple intent surely brings us closer to the presence of our Creator.

Upon receiving the peace prize, Mother Teresa said,

"*I believe that we are not real social workers. We may be doing social work in the eyes of the people, but we are really contemplatives in the heart of the world. For we are touching the body of Christ twenty-four hours....*

And I think that in our family we don't need bombs and guns, to destroy. To bring peace just get together, love one another, bring that peace, that joy, that strength of presence of each other in the home. We will be able to overcome all the evil that is in the world."

The heart of PeaceMakers is the reality that we are all children of the Creator, spiritual children who are very quickly growing up. Much of humanity's struggle for peace arises from not knowing how to mature from childish selfishness into the magnanimous spirit of the sage.

We struggle with division, with separation, judging one as better than another, one right and one wrong, one good and one evil. This struggle becomes the battleground where, from Arjuna's battlefield in the *Baghavad Gita* to the Biblical Armageddon, we come to admit our limitations, change our ways of thinking and behave toward peaceful resolution. Recognizing that we are all spiritual brothers and sisters is the beginning of conscious maturity. This realization seats us in the golden rule taught by every culture on our planet.

In her 1979 acceptance speech, Mother Teresa said,

"And with this prize that I have received as a Prize of Peace, I am going to try to make the home for many people who have no home. Because I believe that love begins at home, and if we can create a home for the poor I think that more and more love will spread. And we will be able through this understanding love to bring peace, be the good news to the poor. The poor in our own family first, in our country, and in the world. ...

"And so let us always meet each other with a smile, for the smile is the beginning of love, and once we begin to love each other naturally we want to do something."[8]

When I finished reading her words, I looked at each person. Everyone sat in silence for a few moments, contemplating her words. Most of us wore a smile on our faces.

I suggested we follow Mother Teresa's advice by experiencing it, right here, right now. I urged each person to find a partner, instructing them to face one another.

Dr. Pam Blosser, a dear friend for years and current President of the School of Metaphysics, and I shared this experience. As I gazed at her, I encouraged others to look at their own partner – and smile!

Giggles filled the air as the initial wave of discomfort swept through most people. This was followed by silence with occasional sighs or laughs or gasps.

I have no idea how long we spent connected in this way, although Mari called it a "ten minute exercise."

When the experience was concluded I suggested people describe what had happened on paper. After about ten minutes I encouraged people to share. What came forth was both soul-stirring and poignant, contemplative and inspirational.

Opening the Curtains
Lisa & Terry's Experience

Dr. Barbara read to us about how Mother Teresa would smile at people first thing (to start the peace) before speaking with them. Dr. Barbara then had us pair off at PeaceMakers and smile as we look into the other person's eyes. I paired off with Terry Martin. At first I started feeling distant. Terry felt very embracing as though she was blanketing me in love. I felt connected, warm, open to receive and at other times I felt very serious. I felt loved, accepted. I wanted to play at times. –Lisa Bold

I've heard that the eyes are the windows to the soul. Now I know that a smile is like opening the curtains to let the light shine out. – Terry Martin

Returning to the Smile We Came From
Paul M & Christine's Experience

Paul Madar remarked, "After a minute or so, the first smile faded. It was a passing smile, courteous, kind, light.

Then came more of me — the smile of liking. I looked into her eyes and saw us both.

This smile faded too, and was reborn as a loving smile. I could tell because my heart jumped, my mind stilled, and I remembered God.

That smile lasted.

As long as I told her 'I love you' that smile lasted. We laughed in distraction, but we both returned to the smile we came from."

Paul's wife Christine experienced one of the most frustrating, and common, thieves of peace, *"I couldn't hold my mind still! These situations are always so uncomfortable for me."* After a few minutes, the busy-ness fades, and as Paul gives more, Christine receives the depth of his love. *"Paul has such kind eyes."*

How Love & Peace will Move across the Earth
Laurie & Paul's experience

S
M
I
L
E

Joyful-Bubbling feeling from my solar plexus chakra area and up. I felt nervousness and then relaxed, tense and relaxed, a pulsation moving closer and closer. Then it was as if everything was illuminated.

As I looked into Paul's eyes his face and body were brilliant. I saw and thought of Gandhi, then I thought, of course he loves the man! I thought about how love moves across the planet by us doing this, looking into one another's eyes and staying with them.

I felt where our two lights became one and then felt connected to all the other people in the room doing the same thing. At that point in time the one became two and the two became many. This is how love and peace will move across the face of the earth simply by facing and smiling with each other.

Love is peace.
It is a smile,
a warm embrace.
It is the sun,
which shines on everyone.
No matter how old, no matter
how young.
No matter how beautiful, no
matter how ugly.
The sun gives.
The son gives.
I am the sun.
I am the son.
Who gives.
Love is the sun.
Peace is the son,
who gives through a smile.
–Laurie Biswell

A smiling face,
warm laugh
Acquaintance known
from lifetimes past
Within your eyes,
the laughing soul
Unhampered, unlimited
complete and whole
A love shared
one for the other
And the other for the one
Two children of
A loving Creation
Children of the Creator,
A Creator who smiles
A Creator who laughs, loves,
embraces!
– Paul Blosser

Soul-to-Soul
Mari & Tad's Experience

When this experience was presented to us and I turned around to look at Tad, one of my classmates, I was happy.

I started laughing in joy at first, and perhaps was a little self-conscious. Then I became calmer and just smiled.

After a few minutes, there was a shift. I felt the smile come from my mind and heart, more deeply. It seemed not important if my mouth showed the smile or not. I did wonder if my mouth was formed in a smile, whether it was or not didn't matter.

What was important was that I recognized how connected I felt with Tad and glad for how far we've come in respect, admiration and caring this year that I have been studying at the College. This was a peace of mind smile.

We smiled soul-to-soul, from the inside out rather than just face-to-face. That's how I want my smiles to always be — very genuine, whole mind smiles reflecting love all the way through. From now on I will give more attention to my smiles and the person I'm smiling with.
–Mari Hamersley

She is curious like a cat.
She tips her head from side to side.
There is a lightness to her being. She is a little uncomfortable and that leads to her laughing nervously. She is a little busy with her thoughts and that leads to laughing.

I thought it is good we are classmates, and looking and smiling at each other.

What is my learning with Mari?

Thank you for the opportunity to learn. When I thought this there was an openness, a calmness, after a while there was a peace I find within my mind! I am connected.

Connected is still. –Tad Messenger

A Cure for the Heart
John & Erika's Experience

As I looked into my friend's eyes I immediately felt a connection that was beyond physical sight. Then what made it even more interesting was that she smiled the whole time I gazed at her face. I smiled as well, and for about what seemed to be ten minutes we concentrated our minds on each other the whole time smiling.

I felt a well spring of joy and warmth come from my heart area as her face glowed with radiance. It kept flowing and I received it. I have been looking for ways to stimulate that warmth in my heart and this exercise was the answer to my prayer.

After a while the physical smile faded and what remained was our mental connection.

I thought to myself that this exercise was a good thing for lovers to do after an argument, or siblings too, when they just can't seem to work together. It is good for anyone who wants peace within themselves and with everyone. It is an instant cure for the heart. –John B. Crainshaw

S
M
I
L
E

I felt a total connection of peace and love. It felt strange at first to keep smiling. I have hidden a smile before, but never kept one on purpose for very long. I connected with the divinity in John Crainshaw, in me, in us. I felt warmth and a "whole mind" love moving between us. The smile was no longer held, but became a natural outflow of the love I felt. I noticed as I sent thoughts of love to John, he would smile bigger. Then I was completely still and received John's presence as a whole Self. It was a beautiful experience. –Erika Scholz

Mirrors of Facets in my Soul
Pam & Barbara's Experience

*Our eyes and smiles settled on each other. The initial smile of beginning
this journey faded and was replaced by a deep appreciation for Dr. Barbara.
I felt this appreciation through my whole being that I could hold in my mind.
I felt it coming out my eyes. I thought of our interactions and what we had
learned living together. I appreciated all the time, the experience, the effort,
the understanding.*

> **Two souls meeting**
> > **face to face.**
> **Agreeing to give**
> > **in a learning embrace.**
> **I'll be for you**
> > **whatever you need**
> **For your karma cleared,**
> > **Your consciousness freed.**
> **I'll play the fool, the mentor**
> > **the child, the mother.**
> **Our learning neatly fitting**
> > **one for the other.**
> **And what we become**
> > **Through understandings gained**
> **Leaves a mark in the cosmos**
> > **of peace that reigns.**
>
> –Pam Blosser

*What struck me first in gazing at Pam was her eyes. My eyes never
left hers. My attention would expand and I realized sometimes her
lips would lift her cheeks in a smile and sometimes her face would
relax in repose. It was the eyes that held me to her and her to me.
"The eyes are the windows of the soul" goes through my head. I
can't remember who said it, and although frustrating, that is not as
important as a sense of knowing what it means.*

I described my experience with Dr. Pam in this way: I was struck by Pam's beauty during this exercise. Physical beauty certainly, a patrician lady in her mid-50s with swanlike neck and Oriental grace, Pam is often striking. It was the beauty of her experiences that resonated with me. Her dharma of attending, how often had she attended me, my hopes, my needs, all the times surfaced at once in my consciousness and I was filled with gratitude. Personal gratitude certainly, yet more than that this was gratitude that we have been able to share the same place on the planet. To occupy the same space with such wonderful accord and rich learning. I felt humbled to know such a great soul, and thankful to call her friend.

Any distance dissolved between us and we breathed together. The thought "I am that I am", surfaced in my mind and I felt the oneness in all creation, that Christ consciousness Mother Teresa talks about.

I then entered into the inner worlds of consciousness, beyond the physical plane. I felt the sadness and tears welled up in my eyes. The reality of separation in the outer world that can create such misunderstandings and barriers to realizing our connection with all of creation. So very glad to have companionship on this journey of learning. Again the gratitude arose and lifted me beyond the polarity, the pairs of opposites, beyond happiness and sadness and all the rest into trust and acceptance and ease.

I knew I was visiting the realm of pure love. My mind was expanding to hold all the elements that make up love. I thought of the lyrics of Dr. Laurel Clark's song *Love Has Many Faces*. This PeaceMaker group had learned it recently and enjoyed singing it.

> *"Love has many faces, I want to know them all.*
> *Beautiful its graces, forever is its call.*
> *In you I see the mirrors of facets in my soul,*
> *brilliant diamonds that once were dark as coal."*

We sang this song before this gathering ended.

Appreciation. Here was the core idea I was coming to understand. In the light of Dr. Pam's love the Biblical thought of blessing came into my mind. "God blessed the seventh day and made it holy, because on it he rested from all the work he had undertaken." Jacob wanting his father's blessing so badly that he would conspire with his mother to steal it from his brother. "Blessed are the Peacemakers, they shall be called children of God." In this moment I understood the connection between blessing and appreciation in a way I had never seen before.

Then my mind went to a story I had read recently about an incredibly wise man.

There was an old, poor man who was envied by kings because he had a beautiful white horse. Kings offered him riches for the horse, but the man would say, "This horse is not a horse to me, he is a person. How can you sell a person, a friend?"

The man was poor, but he never sold the horse.

One morning, the horse was gone. He was not in the stable. The entire village gathered, saying, "You knew someday this would happen old man. Someone has stolen the horse. You should have sold it!"

The old man replied, "Don't jump to conclusions. Merely say the horse is not in the stable. This is the fact; everything else is judgement. Whether it is a misfortune or a blessing I don't know because this is just a fragment. Who knows what is going to follow it?"

People laughed at the old man. They'd always thought him a bit crazy.

After fifteen days, the horse returned. He had not been stolen, he had escaped into the wild. And he had returned with a dozen wild horses!

Again the people gathered and they said, "Old man, you were right. This was not a misfortune, it has indeed proved to be a blessing."

The old man said, "Again you are going to far, jumping to conclusions. Just say that the horse is back. Who knows whether it is a blessing or not? It is only a fragment. You read a single word in a sentence – how can you judge the whole book?"

This time the people could not say much, but inside they knew that he was wrong. Twelve beautiful horses had come....

The old man had an only son who started to train the wild horses. In the first week, he fell from a horse, breaking both legs in the fall. The people gathered again, and again they judged. They said, "Again you proved right! It was a misfortune. Your only son has lost the use of his legs, and in your old age he was your only support. Now you are poorer than ever."

"You are obsessed with judgement. Don't go that far. Say only that my son has broken his legs. Nobody knows whether this is a misfortune or a blessing. Life comes in fragments and more is never given to you."

It happened that after a few weeks the country went to war. All the young men of the town were forcibly taken for the military. Only the old man's son was left, because he was crippled. The whole town was crying and weeping, because it was a losing fight and they knew most of the young people would never come back.

They came to the old man and they said, "You were right, old man– this has proved a blessing. Maybe your son is crippled, but he is still with you. Our sons are gone forever."

The old man said, "You go on and on judging. Nobody knows! Only say this, that your sons have been forced to enter into the army and my son has not been forced. But only God, the total, knows whether it is a blessing or a misfortune."

I could wrap my mind around the concept of being judgement free. Like the man who would not venture to cast judgement, to say one thing is a blessing over another. He would not choose a side, and so remained open to all possibilities, to the infinite.

I was watering the seed that had been planted much earlier in my life. A seed of goodness, acceptance, divine providence. It felt good for that sprout to reach for the sun, bathed by Pam's light. Here, there is freedom, no bondage or slavery or attachment. Here is my resurrection, the realization of Christ.

As I sat drinking in what each person offered, I realized we were experiencing a birth greater than our own newfound awarenesses. John C. said it best, "I think everyone should do this exercise!" My mind immediately moved to fill that need.

"The best way I know to make that happen, is for everyone here to share it, to lead others in the experience," I responded.

"It would be great to put it in a book, so everyone can read it," he replied.

"We can." And that's how this book began on a cold, January Sunday in the hamlet called Windyville where the world's first Peace Dome lives.

Nicholas Zajac

Friendship is

The connection experienced as two (or more) beings,
knowing who and what they really are desire to find common
union on as many levels as they desire. Friendship brings joy
that inspires motion, expansion. It's a self perpetuating circle, much
like the law of prosperity and abundance.

Wholeness is friendship.

Receiving — I receive better (telepathically) with
my mouth open
Giving — **my face hurt from so much smiling** —
I can give my best with undivided attention.

Talina Madonna

Friendship is . . .

**When two or more are Gathered in my
name here I am.**

Beyond words this power flowing through
me from me and into me again and all at
once. Diving Inspiration, Soul Resonance
The Presence of God. Love.
Truth. Holy, Reverent.
Sacrament. The body
and blood of Christ
in you, in me.
Eternal Life.
All One.

Shannon Keener

Love acceptance allowing support able to be with
Timeless   aiding others to fulfill their desires
Namaste

Honoring and respecting the divinity within ourselves and others.
Namaste

Receiving — was very emotional to me. I am so grateful for this
Spiritual Family — I welcome and receive their love fully.

Giving felt so good. I felt an intertwining
of our souls — True communication.

Jonathan Duerbeck

I felt a lot of love and gratitude
and appreciation, and for some reason
some sadness that wasn't really sad.
I thought of a very good friend initially and I
started tearing up and just kept tearing up the
whole time. I felt a little awkward looking into
some people's eyes and I felt some people's
awkwardness. I felt more and more love for each
person and especially people I have formed deep
friendships with. I connected what people
said to my memories and ideals of friendship,
especially toward the friend I miss most now.
Some of what people said was beautiful.
When I spoke I felt like I was giving
from my heart, I felt love.
I wanted to be a better friend.

S
M
I
L
E

Footnotes from Lesson One

1 *Universal Peace Covenant*, ©1997 School of Metaphysics

2 *Prayer for Enlightenment*, amended from World Peace Prayer Society prayer for peace, recited daily at College of Metaphysics.

3 The Words of Peace, ©1990 The Nobel Foundation.

4 Ibid.

5 From the Nobel Peace Prize acceptance speech given by Mother Teresa at Oslo, Norway. © The Nobel Foundation 1979.

6-8 Ibid.

LOVE

Lorena Mary Gregory

Friendship is the love and the faith that you give to know yourself.

I experienced gratitude and the effect of the truth
I have to give that is always present in who I AM.

Friendship
Jaquie 8-3-2003

Is
openly loving, caring, giving, forgiving, togetherness,
openness, never ending, helping one another with
fulfilling desires or doing deeds.
Loving freely and unconditionally,
Just because they are who they are,
Judgement free. Always growing.

Friendship is Loving someone unconditionally, free of limitations.

giving was nice to feel the receiver perceive my thoughts
and feel my spirit rush through the other person receiving.
I felt them take me into them.

receiving was a burst of emotions running through my body.
Very intensely Absorbing another's energies.
Amazing experience taught me to be more receptive
and that was my goal for this weekend.
Thank you.

Lesson Two

LOVE

"Truth resides in the human heart..."

One Sunday afternoon in the year 1949, a young black divinity student traveled to Philadelphia to hear a lecture about Mohandas K. Gandhi, a Hindu religious leader in India who had been assassinated the year before. Gandhi's belief that the power of love is greater than the power of hate, and that love can be used to changed people's ideas and actions made an enduring impression upon the young man.

Before Martin Luther King Jr. read Gandhi's writings, he had almost concluded that the teachings of Jesus could only be put into practice between individuals. After studying the way Gandhi had put his ideas into practice, King realized that he had been mistaken. He wrote, "*Gandhi was probably the first person in history to lift the love ethic of Jesus above mere interaction between individuals to a powerful and effective social force.*"[9]

Six years later Martin Luther King Jr. brought the principles and practices of satyagraha – soul force – to life in the West.

In 1955, a black woman, weary from the day's work, took a Montgomery, Alabama city bus home. Like Gandhi before her, when a man demanded her seat, she refused to give it up. She was arrested and spent the night in jail. The white man's name is long forgotten; the woman's name is Rosa Parks. Her civil disobedience of an unjust law became the spark that ignited the civil rights movement in the United States led by Dr. Martin Luther King Jr. King launched a nonviolent crusade against racial segregation in America, a crusade which eventually earned him the Nobel Peace Prize.

In 1964, King, at 35, became the youngest person to receive the prize. Four years later, he — like his spiritual mentor Gandhi — fell to an assassin's bullet.

What Henry David Thoreau began, Mohandas Gandhi matured. Then, Martin Luther King brought it to fruition. "It" is ahimsa; nonviolence, civil disobedience.

Gandhi did not believe in violence even for the noblest causes. His experiences in England, South Africa, and at home in India had shown him that permanent good is never the outcome of untruth and violence. He saw civil disobedience as an act of conscience—the inherent right of every citizen. He wrote, *"Every state puts down criminal disobedience by force. It perishes, if it does not. But to put down civil disobedience is to attempt to imprison conscience."*[40]

Gandhi gave much thought to these ideas and worked toward ways to implement them. For disobedience to be civil, it *"must be sincere, respectful, restrained, never defiant, must be based upon some well-understood principle."* Above all, civil disobedience must have no ill will or hatred behind it.

"Truth resides in the human heart, and one has to search for it there, and to be guided by truth as one sees it. Satyagraha is the name I gave this new way of overcoming injustice. It means holding on to truth or soul-force."[41]

Gandhi believed evil, injustice, and hatred have no existence of their own. They exist only because we empower them. *"Without our cooperation, unintentional or intentional, injustice cannot continue."* Gandhi saw ahimsa as the great spiritual teaching behind nonviolent non-cooperation.

In his acceptance speech, Dr. King said that ahimsa symbolized *"the spirit and outward form of our encounter."*[42] He believed he received the Nobel prize because as an individual he had become a symbol identified with the struggle for civil rights for Negroes in the United States. He described that struggle as *"taking suffering upon the self instead of inflicting it on others."*

During his acceptance speech for the prize King said,

"In a real sense nonviolence seeks to redeem the spiritual and moral lag (that I spoke of earlier) as the chief dilemma of modern man. It seeks to secure moral ends through moral means. Nonviolence is a powerful and just weapon. Indeed, it is a weapon unique in history, which cuts without wounding and ennobles the man who wields it."[43]

King let it be known that he was accepting the award at a moment when 22 million Negroes were engaged in a creative battle to end racial injustice and establish civil rights. He educated those present that only the day before (receiving the Nobel prize) fire hoses, snarling dogs, and even death met those practicing civil disobedience in Birmingham, Alabama. Others seeking the right to vote in Philadelphia, Mississippi were murdered, and over 40 churches in that state were bombed or burned for rejecting segregation. In light of this he questioned why the prize would be awarded to a movement which had yet to win the peace and brotherhood symbolized by the prize itself.

He accepted the prize as a recognition that nonviolence is the answer to the crucial political and moral question of our time - *"The need for man to overcome oppression and violence without resorting to violence and oppression."* He acknowledged that the Negroes of the U.S., following the people of India, demonstrated that nonviolence is not sterile passivity, but a powerful moral force which makes for social transformation.

"Sooner or later all peoples of the world will have to discover a way to live together in peace, and thereby transform this pending cosmic elegy into a creation psalm of brotherhood. If this is to be achieved man must evolve for all human conflict a method which rejects revenge, aggression and retaliation. The foundation of such a method is love."[4]

I was quite taken with Dr. King's ideas and the way he expressed them. I had been too young when he was doing his work in the world to notice. Now decades later, I could receive the blessing of who he was.

A well read man, King could unite ideas in a powerful way. His influence upon others rose not so much from rhetoric as from his appreciation and employment of imagery in his speeches. He spoke to the inner man, the soul, the Subconscious Mind of all people. This makes his ideas timeless. Half a century later they are as rich, as provocative, as when he spoke them.

Listen to how he describes poverty:

"A second evil which plagues the modern world is that of poverty. Like a monstrous octopus, it projects its nagging, prehensile tentacles in lands and villages all over the world. Almost two-thirds of the peoples of the world go to bed hungry at night."[5]

And this description of mankind's need to understand his own power:

"*Yet, in spite of these spectacular strides in science and technology, and still unlimited ones to come, something basic is missing. There is a sort of poverty of the spirit which stands in glaring contrast to our scientific and technological abundance. The richer we have become materially, the poorer we have become morally and spiritually. We have learned to fly the air like birds and swim the sea like fish, but we have not learned the simple art of living together as brothers.*"[16]

King could take what he had read, the thoughts and ideas of other great thinkers, and weave them together. The result is illuminating discourse that awakens the soul.

"*This call for a worldwide fellowship that lifts neighborly concern beyond one's tribe, race, class, and nation is in reality a call for an all-embracing and unconditional love for all men. This oft misunderstood and misinterpreted concept so readily dismissed by the Nietzsches of the world as a weak and cowardly force, has now become an absolute necessity for the survival of man. When I speak of love I am not speaking of some sentimental and weak response which is little more than emotional bosh. I am speaking of that force which all of the great religions have seen as the supreme unifying principle of life. Love is somehow the key that unlocks the door which leads to ultimate reality. This Hindu-Moslem-Christian-Jewish-Buddhist belief about ultimate reality is beautifully summed up in the First Epistle of Saint John, 'Let us love one another: for love is of God; and everyone that loveth is born of God, and knoweth God'.*" [17]

To experience the truth of what Dr. King said we put: "Love is....." at the top of a sheet of paper. We began writing the thoughts and feelings that surfaced. We described our experience of love.

Although we did not share them at that moment, here are some of them for your consideration.

Tad gave the wonderful perspective of the geologist, "**Love is the movement of energy between matter, in the space of our universe.** It attracts, it binds, it transforms, it creates our universe. It is the movement of energy between two beings that attracts, that connects, that unites and creates interaction, harmony and peace."

John, a computer whiz, noted the vitality of love. "When we are being our real selves, love flows freely causing anything to be possible. It is unifying, healing, and all inclusive. It knows no bounds or limits. It is the energy of life."

Stacy equated love with nature. "Love is like a fire and like a river and like the sun and like a flower and like the rain and like a warm, gentle breeze. Mother Nature knows love best, and she expresses it in all her forms. Sometimes love is moving—fast. Sometimes love is very still—breathing very softly. It is the experience of connecting with truth."

For Mari, Roger's wife and Kira's mom, "**Love is a thought of union with Self, God and others**....Love is our essence and shines brightly on all like the sun. Love is to be given and received. Love is not seen when we are stingy. Love is possible for everyone."

What is Love?

The first thought
I ever had was love.
That thought made
such a splash!
It sent everything
that was still into
motion: mixing, mingling,
intertwining.
After a while I'm sure
everything will settle again
in peace, when everything
that moved from that
first thought realizes
what moved it in the first place.
It's delightful to watch and learn
how love moves, and
how everything responds to it.
I have learned that love
is what causes motion,
and what brings peace.
Love is the only thought
I will ever have.
— Paul Madar

What is Love?

Love is harmony. It is learning to live in peace with ourselves so that we can extend it out to others. When we have violent thoughts about ourselves that is what we manifest. When we live in fear that is what we manifest on a personal and a community or tribal level. Love is experienced in the absence of fear and self hatred. Love is. We do not have to create it. It just is. We create all the other stuff in our insane attempt to deny true love. Love is eternal and it is the word "of creation". Love is more than emotion or feeling. It is connection and bliss, an enveloping transcendence of time and space. Love can be experienced in many ways, but love is not the experience. We can experience love through complete giving and receiving, and I know there is a place beyond the experience, beyond the conscious level of our awareness of that state of being. (Help. Get me out.) Love is the word of creation and the expansion of our being.

— Kerry Leigh

Matthew began with something very real to practicing metaphysicians, "Love is mental connectedness. The ability to unite consciousness and identity with the similarities inherent in each of us. Love is the melody that is produced when I blend with you.

L ight
O f
V alue
E xchanged"

Manager Lisa Bold described love as "an attitude of my mind. It's warm, embracing, and cozy. It's a deep emotional response other than my thoughts. It's giving unconditionally and unselfishly. It's conveying feelings toward other people that you are all for them and value them as an individual."

Medical lab technician Terry echoed these thoughts. "Love is like glue. It's the sticky stuff that connects parent and child, husband and wife. It is what unites all of the leaves to a tree until it's complete. And then love is in releasing so the leaves can blanket the earth becoming substance from which new growth will come. **Love is the un-ending principle for life's evolution.** To be like. Love is light and truth, giving, connecting, being and becoming."

Grade school teacher Erika's response reflected the meaning of friendship, "**Love is the connection between souls.** It is the part of human experience that most profoundly mirrors the divine. Love is why we were brought into being...When all else is removed, love is my true essence."

Web designer Shawn described love in similar ways and then posed the question, "These are some of the things love produces, but what is love itself? It is the attractive force that causes everything from electrons, neutrons, and protons to men and women to planets and moons to galaxies to come together to produce something greater than what was there before in joyful abandon and bliss."

Author Dr. Laurel insightfully offered, "**Love is a verb. Loving is acting as God's messenger.**"

What is Love?

When I had a mediation in which I felt like God and my real Self got together and communicated to me that I was accepted and cared for, that was love.
When my mom and dad raised me and my sister, that was love.
When my teachers teach me, that is love.
When Tina supports people, that is love.
When Paul listens to people, that is love.
When Jesus taught and served, that's love.
Love is a connection, the world is made out of relationships of love.
Love is feeling, being aware of, the connection and putting yourself in alignment with the highest good of another, or even yourself, I suppose.
Love is pro-growth. It accepts and appreciates and cherishes what is loved, in its present state, and helps it grow. There's also a feeling of well-being and harmony and a sense of rightness in love. There's levels of it, too—there's a sliver of love in lust and even tolerance, but it's mixed with other stuff that's not love. The purest love has no desire to get something for the conscious ego, it elevates you because in it you identify with a greater, more connected, more harmonious self. It elevates the lover and the loved. It also is freeing, because when it's pure, you don't need or want anything back and you can't be disappointed, you're just fulfilled and elevated by loving.
Love is.
— Jonathan Deurbeck

L
O
V
E

What is Love?

Love is the inbreath and the outbreath of the Creator, the Creator's thought form and energy moving through us and in us as His children.
Love is His gift to us and our gift to all of Creation which he has entrusted us with.
Love heals. Love manifests. Love connects and fulfills. Love is the vibration of divinity, the song of the Creator playing in all that exists.
Love is personal and universal. It touches heart and mind, body and soul.
It manifests as a person you react to or a life experience that stimulates your mind and heart to open. It is Self-respect. It is listening. It is entrainment. Life is living the life skills and exemplifying the great masters.
Love is who I Am. Love is who you are. Love is what we are to be. Love is why we are most important to each other—as facets and points of light of one Creation.

— Paul Blosser

College instructor Dr. Pam described the experience of love in action eloquently. "It can be heard in a mother's cooing to her baby. It can be seen in the sacrifice for something greater than the Self. It can be smelled when true friends meet and share learning and growth. It can be tasted when a child runs to gleefully hug another. It can be felt in a touch, a glance, a smile, a caress. **Love is a movement from the infinite source through all the hearts of creation**."

Minister Teresa Padilla gave us images of this Source. "Love is the voice of God echoed through the sounds of nature and received through open minds who can hear. It is the eyes of God reflected through the window of our soul, and captured by one still, respectful mind who is ready to see. It is the breath of God, received fully by the entrained mind, expectantly."

Writing of cycles, I concluded my thoughts with "Love is both the need and the fulfillment, the male and the female, birth and death. I am loved and beloved, resurrected."

Describing our thoughts about love was just the beginning of this exercise. Now we would join in an experience of love. There were 20 people present, so we divided into two groups. One group became the inner circle, standing shoulder-to-shoulder forming a circle, facing outward. The second group circled the first, forming an outer ring standing side-by-side facing inward. Each person thus faced another.

Instructions were given for the inner circle people to form one sentence that exemplified their idea of "love is...." Few words, much detail. The experience began when everyone in the inner circle stated aloud to the person facing them, "Love is....." and they finished the sentence. This occurred simultaneously. When silence rose, the inner circle rotated so each participant could move on to the next person and repeat his or her insight. This continued until all ten had spoken their statements on love.

Those receiving – those in the outer circle held their minds still during this exercise – drinking in the love offered by the others.

Upon completion everyone wrote about their experience. The inner circle wrote about their experience of giving. The outer circle wrote of their experience of receiving.

Then the groups came back together this time switching places so the givers were now receivers, and

What is Love?

1. **Love = evolve**
2. **Connectedness**
3. **Light**
4. **Connectedness in Light**
5. **Drawing power**
6. **The receptive factor of creation**
7. **A feel good sensation**
8. **An emotional nicety - joy**
9. **An aligning experience**
10. **A peace filled being**
11. **An exhilarating experience**
12. **A very powerful teaching quality**
13. **Caring**

— **Dr. Daniel Condron**

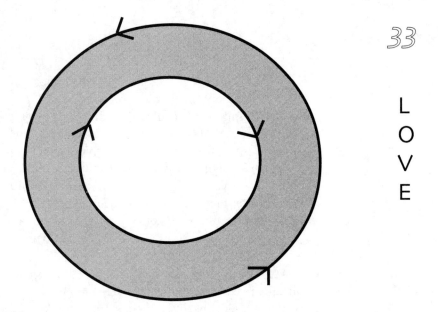

the receivers became givers. In this way by the end of the exercise every-one had given and received from each person present. The glow emanated from each of us. How our awareness of love was growing clearly reflected in our faces.

Here is how we described our experience in words.

PeaceMakers, Sunday, January 19, 2003

Reflections from Dr. Daniel Condron's experience

Receiving Love
> Love is the Blessing of the universe.
> Love is the freedom to receive.
> Love is the joy of oneness.
> Love is the peace of connectedness.

Giving Love
> "Love is my golden-hearted act of giving."
> I gave my love.
> I experienced people receiving my love.
> I shared my love.

Reflections from Dr. Laurel Clark's Experience

Giving Love

When I was giving, I felt the kind of anticipation I do on Christmas morning, looking forward to giving to each person. After the first couple of times it seemed like we all moved in sync—it took a couple of times for all the givers to move together as a wheel, like a chakra. Giving was fulfilling, especially when my mental image was clear and distinct. (Sometimes I got distracted by the loud voice next to me and felt like I was losing myself — like a drop of water in an ocean.) I realized later that the "in sync" occurred as I expanded my consciousness so that I could be centered in my Self in relationship to the whole, like being a spoke in a wheel.

Receiving Love

When I was receiving, I enjoyed the stillness and allowed myself to breathe in each person who gave to me. It was as if they were giving themselves to me, not just an idea. I felt moved to tears.

Reflections from Lisa Bold's experience

Receiving Love

I felt everyone was very open to what love is to them. The picture I got was one of connectedness and God's love moving through all of us with open arms.

Giving love

Everyone seems really receptive and open. I felt loved and connected.

.Reflections from Paul Madar's experience

Receiving Love

Mostly I received the thought that Love is the energy of the Creator moving through everything. I also received a picture of Love being bright, flowing, permeating, and connecting everything together. I tried remembering each thought at first, then simply let all of them wash through me to grasp the universal.

Giving Love

I felt like a wise master-teacher passing on the wisdom of the saints, and then felt everyone else in the inner circle sending out their picture, too. That felt like a sun radiating out rays of Light, all different expressions of Love, all true, yet each is different— like the birth of I AMs.

LOVE

Reflections from John Harrison's experience

Receiving Love

I received many different views of love. Some matched my own, many included what I believed. Love is energy, it connects us with each other, it is involved with or in Creation. When receiving from Dr. Laurel I felt my heart chakra spin or flutter or become agitated the most. With Matthew I felt his energy reaching out, trying to connect with me.

Giving Love

In giving I attempted to allow myself to give my love and light. Some made it out but not as far out as I would have liked. I was still holding back and trying to protect myself. Everyone was pretty open and receptive. I found I had (or I initiated) sounding a "gong-ding" to cause everyone to move to the next person. I had to be aggressive. I felt I needed to wait longer between each one to let the message and the love sink into each person before moving on.

Reflections from Terry Martin's experience

Receiving Love

At first I wanted to give back by nodding or doing something physically. I noticed this was stronger when I believed or sensed some discomfort within the person giving. I wanted to create within myself an opening to fully receive and so I breathed with the person giving.

Giving Love

I had a clear thought of love and it was easy to give. I experienced connectedness all the way through myself no matter who I was giving to.

Reflections from Matthew Marian's experience

Giving Love

The thought I gave to everyone in the circle is "love is mental connectedness." As I gazed at the people who were receiving me I realized this is the experience of love. Every time I am with someone I have an opportunity to practice. It is so simple to reach out and embrace each other mentally. I imagine my experience of love to deepen and grow as I give and receive.

Receiving Love

I felt connected. I smiled the whole time. Everyone has an image of love and the most valuable aspect of the experience was they gave it to me and I received it. It is amazing to think of life as being that simple. What I mean is that I think we are all here to give and receive love.

Reflections from Sharka Glet's experience

Giving Love

"Love is this wonderful, warm creative energy. We all are made out of this energy and it is Peachy Pink."

I loved describing love. Each time I said the sentence the picture of love became clearer in my mind and my heart became bubbly happy.

Receiving Love

I wish I remembered all what I have received. I have received a big bundle of warm energy through the attention of the individuals. I saw all the different attentions being connected to one source of light.

Reflections from Kerry Leigh's experience

Receiving Love

It was an experience that opened up my heart to hear what was being given. I experienced a connection with each person that expanded to include everyone in the room and beyond. Being receptive allowed me to let go of the past and just be present in this lovely moment, listening, and receiving is giving.

Giving Love

Giving my vision to another was experienced by me as gratefulness for their presence and their receptivity and openness. Love is universal and universally exists so it is good to be able to give without fear. I received the benefit.

Reflections from Stacy Ann Ferguson's experience

Giving Love

I said to everyone who was receiving that "Love is a fountain of giving." As I went around the circle, I felt like a fountain. I smiled so much. The love I felt was so intense that I had a hard time containing it. I wanted to touch or hug everyone.

Receiving Love

That was so intense. I could barely handle it. I felt like the sun, radiating with enough energy to cause and sustain life in countless forms. Very warm light expanding to infinity. A glimpse of nirvana. Each person was like Buddha.

Reflections from Barbara Condron's experience

Receiving Love

I expanded as each new wave filled my being — the cosmic Christ. Energy, power, connection, breath, God unites. Radiant energy — image Universal energy — complete. Free enduring, continuous. I experience breath of God.

Giving Love

Living, breathing with God. Image is the same as when receiving — as if different part lights up with each person. Acknowledgement of this light is reflected in the voice — in how I convey the thought — energy, inflection, emphasis — with each. This is the truth of "Love ye one another." The melody of an unfinished song I started several years ago came into my mind. The song's title – "Love ye one another."

L
O
V
E

Reflections from Paul Blosser's experience

Giving Love

"Love is the energy of the Creator moving through us to all of Creation." I formed a mental picture of our planet bathed in the light and love of Creation so everyone and everything was bathed in this Light and Love. By giving this thought form, I experienced openness with each person and a connectedness. I formed the thought in my mind, said the thought and then formed a picture again.

Receiving Love

I stilled my mind to receive each person and their idea of love. Love is glue, it is energy, it is within each of us, moving from the Creator to us throughout the universe. It is inclusive, expansive, infinite, connected. It is our golden opportunity to be like our Creator.

Reflections from Erika Scholz's experience

Receiving Love

It was really inspiring to receive people's images of love. I saw love through each of their eyes. I felt heart-centered and connected as I received each of their images. What Jonathan said really touched me because of its "humanness." I also really appreciated Tad's view of love. Each person became a facet of love that I was shown.

Giving Love

I said, "Love is my truest manifestation of divinity." As I said this, I felt it resonate through me. I saw God in each of the recipient's faces. I felt divine love pass between us. It was beautiful.

Reflections from Laurie J. Biswell's experience

Giving Love

"Love is a powerful unifying energy that connects us all,
God and humanity."
It took me awhile to commit to a sentence. I felt nervous and very awkward willing to give. My solar plexus, and I probably recognize this the
strongest since this is what I am studying now, was tingling, pulsating. I
felt and acted like I couldn't sit still to energy just rushing like I have to
move, dance, cannot sit still, rhythmically up and down.

Receiving Love

I felt calmer, more relaxed, open every once in a while. I would still feel
the bubbling pulsation of energy that needed to spew out, go forth from
somewhere. Smiling faces connecting as the circle moved I noticed each
sentence of "what is...." was different, as different as each individual
expression. The core of love is the same, that love is all.

Reflections from Mari Hamersley's experience

Receiving Love

I received each person giving their picture of love. I was still and
listened to their words and at times formed an image in my mind. The
most important part was simply being with that person who gave,
looking in their eyes and loving them, receiving the essence of who they
are, truly connecting in love.

Giving Love

As I gave, I said, "Love is the light and the energy of the Creator touching us all." After I said that I moved God's energy through me and
mentally embraced each person. I wanted to stay there with each of
them and experience the love, be one with them a little longer until it felt
natural to move on. "Let me stay," I thought. Then I remembered that
we're always connected in love. Then I experienced peace.
Ahhh...Truth.

Reflections from Teresa Padilla's experience

Giving Love

I was endeavoring to give what was moving through me in that moment.
I experienced my picture being added to through the pictures of those
around me. So what I had to say changed as I continued to give. I
experienced the connection of others and how this effects and adds to me
each moment.

Receiving Love

It was easier for me to receive. I was more centered. I felt warm, at
peace, loved, appreciation for all of us. I experienced oneness. I was
experiencing bubbles of joy welling up within.

Reflections from Tad Messenger's experience

Giving Love

Giving my thought of what is love made that thought clear in my mind and opened my mind to the multidimensional facets of love. It made sense. Giving it many times made it crystallize in my mind.

Receiving Love

I received love from the giver as they gave their thought of what is love? Many facets including the Creator's thought.

Mirrors of love move across my mind.

Fountains of love pour into my heart.

Love is all around, love is everywhere and kind.

Love is where the universe connected at the start.

L
O
V
E

Reflections from Jonathan Duerbeck's experience

Giving Love

I believed in what I said.

Love is awareness of connection with what is loved and accepting and cherishing it as it is now and aiding it to grow, elevating the lover in the process. I stand far accepting and appreciating and aiding growth. That's the big part. I felt nervous telling Doctors of Metaphysics what love is. I felt like saying "I think" or "I believe" first. I felt kind of canned a few times.

Receiving Love

I felt awkward in the silence after listening sometimes. I wanted more time to let it sink in, all those profound ideas or profound truths. It gave me a self-respect of seeing how other people define love is different than how I do. Different views of it stand out to different people, and it's still the same thing and it all fits together. Unity in diversity.

Reflections from Shawn Stoner's experience

Giving Love

Giving my picture of love was still, connected. At first there were giggles, but these subsided and in their place was a strong picture and a deep desire to connect with the person I was giving to. My thought would move through me and I could feel it like a wave moving toward the other person.

Receiving Love

Receiving was a cosmic experience — like receiving the thoughts of God. I had to be still — the power of the thoughts were so strong. Each picture had at its essence the essence of the one who gave it,

Reflections from Dr. Pamela Blosser's experience

Receiving Love

> I received joy
> > childlikeness
> like an infant
> beauty
> each seemed like a child who
> > had made a discovery
> > that was the most important
> > thing to them.
> I received each person
> > their thoughts, their glee
> > their nervousness, their love.

Giving Love

For about half way I had not formulated a clear image so what I gave was incomplete. When I found the clear thought I could feel a connection with the other, and them receiving what I said. With Laurel I could see the thought going into her.

My ideas of love have changed again and again and again since I began practicing metaphysics. The unconditional love shown by SOM teachers and students toward a new person - me - was one of the first validations that I was in the right place. I had always dreamed such acceptance was possible. I believed it existed. And here it was in Columbia, Missouri!

The School also teaches one of the best tools for developing a loving, connected consciousness. We call it a circle of love. This circle creates, shares, and projects light and love between individuals and with all of humankind. At the close the words "I love you just because you are" are passed from one person to the next.

"I love you just because you are." No conditions. No exclusions. Regardless of social class, color of skin, philosophies, emotions, and the like. This love expresses just because you exist. This is namaskar, honoring another's existence. It is the deepest form of respect and the fullest experience of love.

I have come to see the Circle of Love as a joyous moment of awakening for many. The personal growth that enables someone to look a stranger in the eyes and say "I love you just because you are" and mean it, is inspiring. With each successive opportunity, you can easily evaluate where you have come from, where you are, and image where you can go.

The Circle of Love has spread into churches and groups through the years, as students have taken it into the world. It is a good seed, a way to love one another, and it is growing in the hearts of men, women, and children around the world.

Carrie Collins

Friendship is Complete and open communication
and giving and receiving **with love in your heart
and truth in your mind**.

My experience was I was more comfortable and at ease with
giving and a little uncentered when receiving.

I felt in my heart that just by saying those things friendship
deepened, connections were made even with people I just met
this weekend that I hadn't even talked with before.

What I received was that friendship is the goodness
for all concerned, connectedness and love.

Dave Rosemann

Friendship is loving and accepting others
Friendship is being connected wherever you are
Friendship is always being open to others
Friendship is sharing ideas. Friendship is a warm smile
Friendship is giving someone a hug when they need it or even if
they don't.

Friendship is an open connection with others wherever you are.

I felt like I was giving Truth to each individual. I could see that
each person received it uniquely.

In receiving I felt like I was receiving truth from
each person. I could feel my chakras whirling as
they were energized with these thoughts.

What is Friendship?
Jason J Sucec

Friendship in connection with another, it is sharing
openly & honestly in love.

Connection with others through sharing openly; honestly in Love.

My experience with giving Friendship to others was connection
soul to soul, playful, Loving & open.

Profound ... New ... Feeling inside through outside.

My experience in receiving
thankfulness, caring, connection. Crying joyfully
in deep connection with another soul.

Footnotes from *Lesson Two*

9 From Presentation Speech honoring Dr. Martin Luther King, Jr. with the Nobel Peace Prize by Junnar John, chairman of the Nobel Committee, Dec. 11, 1964. Taken from Dr. King's writings. © The Nobel Foundation, 1964.

10 From **Gandhi: The Man** by Eknath Easwaran © 1972 by Blue Mountain Center of Meditation. Nilgiri Press.

11 Ibid.

12 Martin Luther King, Jr.'s acceptance speech "The Quest for Peace and Justice" © The Nobel Foundation 1964

13-17 Ibid.

Lesson Three

RESPECT

*"The only force
 which can break down those barriers
 is the force of love, the force of truth,*

soul force."

Chance Cannon

Friendship is
the giving and receiving of truth with love being perfectly
imperfect with **complete acceptance of one another**.

I tried to connect to each person's soul.
To receive and then give, soul to soul.

What is friendship?
Judy Weber

Being able to care enough about a person or people
to recognize when they are happy / sad — whatever and
being able & willing to respond to that — But also, when you
have differences of opinion, or feel you have been wronged or
misunderstood. To with the purpose of maintaining a friendship
and to stick with it until you can understand each other.

Self respecting yourself and your friend

Receiving —
Statements were so beautiful I felt wonderful energy and love
from heartfelt statements.

Giving —
I learned I need to self respect more as I didn't feel
my statement was deep enough — I also had pleasure
in sending energy of love to people who were
receiving & could feel acceptance and love
from those who received.

This Sunday our numbers more than doubled. Students from Columbia who would be receiving their Past Life Profiles following lunch had come early for the purpose of joining us at our peacemakers gathering.

I had chosen two women for this morning's contemplation and discussion. Betty Williams and Mairead Corrigan. The way these two women came together changed them and the world.

One day in August 1976 in a working-class neighborhood in Belfast, Northern Ireland, a getaway car driven by a member of the Irish Republican Army (IRA) went out of control and crashed into an iron railing, killing three young children and seriously injuring their mother. Betty Williams witnessed the tragedy. Horrified, she immediately began collecting signatures on a petition calling for an end to hostilities between the IRA and the British-controlled government of North Ireland.

The sister of the injured woman, aunt of the three dead children was Mairead Corrigan.

On the day of the funeral, these two Roman Catholic secretaries who never finished secondary school, organized a protest march. Ten thousand women marched from Andersontown where the deaths occurred to the grave sites. In this simple action a peace movement was launched that resulted a year later in the awarding of the Nobel Peace Prize to Corrigan and Williams.

The origins of "the troubles" as the Irish call their long civil war in the north reach as far back as the first invasions of Ireland by the English in the 12th century. Natives have always resisted British rule, and since the 1800s the Irish Republican Army has spearheaded the independence efforts. In 1921 the country was divided, southern Ireland became a free country in 1948. Northern Ireland remains a part of the United Kingdom.

With the help of Ciaran McKeown, a journalist, Williams and Corrigan founded Peace People. They were praised by the Nobel committee for giving "fresh hope to people who believed that all hope was gone." Their work with Peace People included programs to help survivors of terrorist attacks, assist victims of violence in claiming compensation from the government, build community centers in poor neighborhoods, and restore damaged businesses and schools. They also sponsored a campaign in which terrorists were persuaded to surrender their weapons.

Today both women continue to work for peace. Corrigan-Maguire (now remarried) continues as director of an allied organization, Peace People's Commitment to Active Non-violence, and Williams from her home in America.

Betty Williams traveled to Norway to receive the prize on behalf of herself and Corrigan. Her acceptance speech reminded us of what we had learned the previous week about the power of love. Speaking about the Peace People she said that they believe in removing barriers and reconciling people through getting to know each other, talking each other's languages, understanding each other's fears and beliefs. She advocated getting to know people physically, philosophically, and spiritually. *"It is much harder to kill your near neighbor than the thousands of unknown and hostile aliens at the other end of a nuclear missile. We have to create a world in which there are no unknown, hostile aliens at the other end of any missiles,"* she said that day in Oslo.[18]

To those who believe this a good idea but lack the imagination to determine how, Betty had an answer, *"The only force which can break down those barriers is the force of love, the force of truth, soul force."* Deeply influenced by the earlier work of Dr. Martin Luther King, Jr., Betty was passionately dedicated to the cause of nonviolence.

"To those who say that we are naive, utopian idealists, we say that we are the only realists, and that those who continue to support militarism in our time are supporting the progress towards total self-destruction of the human race, when the only right and left will be dead to the right and dead to the left, and death and destruction right, left, and center, east and west, north and south. We wish to see those who keep the lights burning twenty-four hours a day in the Pentagon and the Kremlin and all the other great centers of militarism liberated into truly creative and happy lives instead of the soul-destroying tasks of preparing for self-destruction."

Betty's passion now had a focus that changed her world and ours. *The Declaration of the Peace People* states:

We have a simple message for the world from this movement for peace.

We want to live and love and build a just and peaceful society.

We want for our children, as we want for ourselves, lives at home, at work and at play to be lives of joy and peace.

We recognize that to build such a life demands of all of us dedication, hard work and courage.

We recognize that there are many problems in our society which are a source of conflict and violence.

We recognize that every bullet fired and every exploding bomb makes that work more difficult.

We reject the use of the bomb and the bullet and all the techniques of violence.

We dedicate ourselves to working with our neighbors, near and far, day in and day out, to building that peaceful society in which the tragedies we have known are a bad memory and a continuing warning."

Being on that Belfast street on that day in August was a defining moment for Betty Williams. She made the choice to make a difference. We each have opportunities to experience these epiphanies. There are times when life seems to pick us up and places us in a completely new position, a new point of view from which life seems very different. This was the thought project of the morning – to identify a defining moment in our own lives that has made all the difference.

We searched through the memories of experiences that have made us the people we are and we wrote about them. Some, like Dr. Daniel, listed several experiences, others, like Erika, described a single experience. What was certain, this morning we were focused upon identifying first the experience, then our thoughts about the experience which caused us to see ourselves, our lives, and others in an illuminating way.

Here are our stories of the events that molded, and sometimes changed, our lives.

What Fashions a Man by Daniel R. Condron

1. Helping the adult men in the hay field driving a tractor
2. Playing basketball and leading the team
3. Tractor and wagon rolling backwards down hill
4. Frying an egg sandwich for my mother
5. Making a pen for the hogs in the barn so they wouldn't freeze
6. Ordering and planting fruit trees on the farm I grew up on
7. Planting pine trees there
8. Going to college
9. Being in a fraternity
10. Graduating from college
11. Going to South America for data collection of my masters thesis
12. Entering the School of Metaphysics
13. When I said to myself about the University of Missouri-
    I have learned everything I can learn here
14. When I made the choice to move to Des Moines to a
    new SOM Center instead of Washington, D.C. for a job

Yearning for Experience by Stacy Ann Ferguson

The times when I speak to an individual or a group, especially a group and I share a vision of what is and can be. The times I give more love and compassion and forgiveness than is expected. At those times I feel a shift in myself and others. There is an elevation, a new grasp of truth, of the beauty within us waiting to be brought forth. The times I give my love and attention to a stranger and connect with them as a soul. In that moment the connectedness that can be with everyone everywhere is illumined for both.

Public Speaking by Terry Martin

I was 16 and had written a paper that was selected as one of the three finalists in the area. I hadn't realized the three finalists would need to present their papers in front of groups but since I'd won I had to go through with the next step. I visualized myself presenting the paper and answering their questions. I believed if I could do this in my mind I would be able to present the paper and be okay speaking in front of people.

Divine Intervention by John Mestyanek

I was in my best friend's room, and we were relaxing on the couch. An alien poster on his wall came to life. It communicated with us how we as humans have the physical form that we do. This was shown to us through images of the aliens mixing with the primitive life on the planet. I was also shown where I would be taken if I continued to pursue the lifestyle I was currently living. I didn't find this very attractive.

Another defining moment was when I hitchhiked from Florida to Texas. I was coming from a commune that I decided to leave because they didn't believe in God. I wanted this experience to be one of reconnecting with God. On my journey, the first night it was getting dark and I was about to cross this overpass when someone called out to me. It was this couple that had food and a blanket and the lady prayed over me for God to protect me. The next night it was already dark and I was about to give up on the thought of anyone picking me up when a mini van pulled over. It ended up the guy driving was a youth minister and he drove me all the way to Lafayette. He helped pay for me to get a room and prayed for me before he left. The next day my sister picked me up in Houston.

R
E
S
P
E
C
T

Finding Your Voice by Lisa Bold

I remember in high school a lot of girls in the locker room were talking about my next door neighbor who I knew well. He was stood up for a dance and the girls were talking about it. They were talking about him as if he was this big monster. All this was based off of one person (the girl who stood him up). None of what she said was true and a lot of girls were talking about him like they knew from personal experience. I hesitated on saying any-thing because I wanted everyone to like me. I got to a point where I had to speak out and let everyone know my experience of my next door neighbor-that he was a great, loving guy. A couple of the girls came up to me later and said they felt bad about going with the flow. I knew this had an effect on my neighbor in the years to come. This was a defining moment for me on standing on what I knew to be right and knowing my voice can make a difference.

Becoming Somebody *by John Crainshaw*

January 1, 1998 Universal Hour of Peace-connected with all of creation around the peace pole with the people who lived at COM.

January 1, 1996, going through Crown Center, Kansas City at New Years with Brock and Tony. Knew so much change was coming. Found SOM 3 months later. Also that night found the brochure for the lecture I went to by SOM at UMKC. Found it at the Daily Grind.

July 1996 at SOMA reunion campout. After Little Gerry's talk had the most amazing dream ever.

September 1993-Performed music at my junior high talent show. Everyone cheered. Before that I was a nobody. 3 years earlier set a desire into motion that I would bring the wonders of music to the world.

New Start *by Teresa Padilla*

This moment was when I recognized an unexpressed struggle of blame, resentment, and despair. I surrendered by admitting my thoughts about leaving the School. I received the truth, love, and support. I came to know what I would gain by surrendering my little self completely to my inner desire for strength, love, and commitment. I decided to stay in SOM and to be a field director.

Roads Taken *by Luke Mulderink*

Defining Moment: A moment that helped me to become who I am today. Breaking with Bill O-cause of breaking with Bill. Going to Wortern. Depression-cause of depression? Always had those thoughts. Decision not to drink. Who am I today? Spiritual, semi-musical, philosophical, confused, empowered. What caused my conscious awareness? Why do I do what I feel others would think they should do? Move to Columbia. Needed to talk with the wise. Decision to change major-defining moment. Depressed, unathletic, sulky, sulky, learned that I was feeling, stepped outside, grasped consciousness, filled with bliss, then I was on spiritual path. Decision to do exercises every day-decided to take control of my life and consciousness. Want to contribute my thoughts to the whole, get them out, see what they think.

All Experiences of Life Lead to One Moment
by Matthew Marian

I walked up the steps of a porch that stretched across the front of a warm and welcoming building. I walked into the living room of this building and sat down on the couch. A young woman came and brought me some tea. More people arrived, there was some polite chit-chat.

An older man I had seen upon entering the building came into the living room and began talking to us. He talked about how to answer questions, questions like what is the purpose of life, who are we, and where do we come from. No one had ever talked to me about the answers to these questions and he didn't either. The man told me I could learn how to answer those questions for myself.

All the experiences of my life led me to that moment in time. All of my frustration, fighting, anxiety, and pain were the crucible that prepared me to begin transcending everything that has ever held me back or limited me. This moment was the culmination of ages of preparation and the beginning of eternity.

The Power of Intuition *by Christine Madar*

-First time I heard an intuitive report
-First time I saw reports done
-The experience of the stillbirth
-When Dr. Barbara asked if I would like to lead the delegation to India
-The first time I met Paul Madar at the College of Metaphysics
-Giving a sermon after September 11th
-Receiving my dharma report
-Living in Ireland, our trip to the north and seeing an occupied country, surveillance cameras, armed men-watching a mother with her baby walk in front of a soldier who had his gun trained on something-she seemed indifferent-people live this way around the world

Challenge of Physical Limitations of the Body
*by **Dave Rosemann***
-Hiking with my father and my Boy Scout troop.
One of the hardest things I ever did and I really expanded
beyond many limitations.
-The first time I was in the hospital and
I got my heel cord transfer done.
-When I had both legs in casts and had some
difficult but growth-filled learning experiences.
-Doing the ropes course at 40 legends
-College Forum '97 experience of connecting with campers
-Becoming a student at the School of Metaphysics

Soul Travel *by **Paul Madar***

I can think of many defining moments in my life, moments when my decisions, choices, and response altered the course of my life permanently. One of the earliest moments came right after high school. I had decided to travel across the U.S. to California and live there for a while. I had in mind that it was to be a spiritual journey to discover deeper truths of the universe and myself.

I packed many books about tibetan monastic life, thinking they would rub off, into my old Ford Maverick and proceeded to hop from state beach to state beach in California. I read voraciously and in the process decided I wanted to experience first-hand causing myself to leave my body—to astral project.

I had a manual of sorts, of how to do it, and I followed the instructions religiously every night. I felt the itching, the rushing sounds, the twitches, the breathing. I moved my attention far above my body, but I still wasn't able to separate.

Finally, while visiting a friend's house and staying overnight, it happened. I did my usual practice of relaxing and breathing. All of a sudden I flew through a mental tunnel of light and sound and emerged at the ceiling. At that point I came to know I am a soul and I had to learn the "secrets of life". Ever since then I have been adding to that awareness, that experience, that knowing, and one way or another teaching it to others.

The Mind Opens *by Pam Blosser*

Going to state commission while in high school opened my mind to greater possibilities of learning. Key note speaker was Bill Smith, Episcopal minister, his mind was so open that his visions stimulated me greatly. Bill Smith introduced me to a great thinker who delved into ideas of consciousness and spirituality. I returned with greater commitment to my spiritual growth. I think of this moment every time we have Camp Niangua because it reminds me how much can happen in a short time and how people's lives and consciousness can be changed if their minds are open and the stimulus is profound and penetrating. The experiences that are created for them at camp have changed the camper's lives on many levels, from enjoying reading, to eating more and different kinds of food, to volunteering to help others or being more independent and assertive. From understanding true friendship to the entering into expansive realms of peace.

R
E
S
P
E
C
T

How We Influence Others *by John Harrison*

1. I was at my Christmas floor party in college. A girl wanted to dance with me but I refused because I really didn't know how, and was insecure doing it. She ran off crying. I and another person went after her. We caught up to her outside. It was pretty cold. I explained why I refused. She thought it was because I didn't like her but that wasn't the case. She ended up by giving me a hug and a kiss on the cheek.

2. I was up in the chapel at the College of Metaphysics. I had just arrived and was talking to several people. I noticed Bernadette laying on her bed. She had graduated her year at the College and I was overjoyed at seeing her. I didn't want to make her get up to give me a hug so I made a big fuss about being glad to see her and I just had to touch her and be around her. She was very pleased and smiled. It is one of the first instances when I noticed my dharma quality of warmth come out.

Different Choices *by Carrie Collins*

-Parent's divorce
-Dream when I was 13
*Experience on my 22nd birthday
-Found the School

*I had done a combination of drugs and experienced going very deep within. Falling and falling and falling until I stopped and was just suspended in a timeless eternal now. I saw all the choices I had made in all my past lives led to what I was experiencing now and at that time I wasn't even sure if I believed in reincarnation, and then if I was to keep making the same kind of choices where it would lead me and that I was very important the reason I am here this lifetime is very important and I needed to make different choices and then I saw the universe from above and saw how there was order and all the Universal Laws working together. After that I immediately made different choices and had several wonderful experiences like the precognitive dream and a few months later I found the School.

Charisma *by Tad Messenger*

Giving a sermon at my church entitled "The First Third of Your Life" when I was 16 years old. I had had several moments in my early life where I had the opportunity to speak in front of a large group of people. I had experienced much emotional turmoil and fear. One time I had thrown up on a grand piano that was backstage. I would always get sick to my stomach.

When I gave the sermon I was especially nervous. However this time I was filled with love for the people in the church and I had something I wanted to give. My thoughts were on giving. I experienced great joy, excitement, and power as I gave the sermon at both the 9 and 11 services. This was a defining moment because it was my first experience of the power of giving and my first experience of recognizing my desire to be a spiritual leader. There was so much I received from giving. I recognized I had charisma by giving love.

I clearly saw that spiritual life was the most important quest for me. I heard authority and spiritual leader in my voice.

Time *by Carol Gunn*

1. The day I took my first drink.
2. The day I found out my dad was not my father.
3. The day I let Terry beat Cyrus.
4. The day I found out I was pregnant.
5. The day I read, <u>Fear of Flying</u> and decided I could leave Pat.
6. The day I married Terry.
7. The day I divorced Terry.
8. The day I came to the School of Metaphysics.
9. The days I gave birth to each of my babies.
10. The day I decided to get sober.
11. The day I took Joshua to my brother's and then came back home.
12. The day Noah went to jail.

R
E
S
P
E
C
T

Influential People *by Nancy Minter*

1. In high school when my father told me I was capable of doing whatever I wanted to do.
2. In San Diego when I realized, by a statement made by a friend, that my perception of myself and other's perceptions of me were very different.
3. When I chose to marry my husband and realized my vision of the future was a possibility.
4. When my son Michael was born and I saw the incredible amount of love that I was capable of giving to another.
5. When I made a statement to my sister that I believed in reincarnation and my husband reacted so strongly that I was put in a position of defending my beliefs. I realized I wanted to pursue this direction more fully.
6. When I met a friend who had ideas that were metaphysical in nature and caused an awakening and desire for knowledge I didn't even realize I was lacking.
7. Becoming a student at the School of Metaphysics.

Holding to Ideals by *Laurel Clark*

This is kind of hard to identify. In stages of growth:

Infancy

When I went to school, I was surprised and hurt by the ways that kids were mean to each other and ridiculed each other. I had not experienced that before. In kindergarten I remember lying in bed, crying and agonizing over something that had happened that day. One of the boys in the class was called a sissy and teased for playing with the great dollhouse in the classroom. I could feel his pain and felt powerless to do anything about it.

When I was in 3rd grade, there was a similar event. Sharon Greenblatt was one of the girls in the class. She was physically unattractive, like the ugly duckling. Some of the kids in the class made up a game, saying that if anyone stepped on the green or black squares (the tile floor of the classroom had beige green and black squares) they had the "greenblatts" which meant they were poisoned. Sharon was in tears. I felt terrible but I didn't know what to do. Although I was painfully shy myself, I said I wasn't going to play the game because it was mean. When I said that, some of the other kids followed my lead. Sharon and I became friends after that. I learned I could be an example and hold true to my ideals even when it was not popular. I also learned I could make a difference by doing what I believed was the right thing to do.

Adolescence

I was valedictorian of my high school class of about 750 students. I graduated 6 months early, in January rather than June, so I had many months to think about a speech for the graduation ceremony. At first I wasn't planning to attend the ceremony until my mother said in a shocked voice that I needed to give the speech. That stimulated me to think about the importance of giving what I thought was a key message for the graduating class to have. Some of my reluctance to give a speech was because I knew that up until 10th grade I had really tried to do my best in school, but during 10th grade I had become somewhat rebellious, started smoking pot, and had learned that I could still get good grades without putting out my best effort. So I was actually surprised when I found out I was valedictorian and felt kind of guilty about it.

That stimulated me to think about what it even meant to be valedictorian, that it was based on grades and not on learning, and that the real value of education was in the learning. That's really what I was disappointed about—that I had let myself down in the last year and a half of high school and hadn't challenged myself. So I wrote the speech about the idea that school is supposed to be for learning, and that grades don't necessarily reflect what you have learned, they reflect how well you have pleased your teachers. I practiced the speech in my mind many times, over and over. I pictured what I wanted to say. I was moved to give this message because I wanted to reform the school system! I think I also wanted to shock people into paying attention, although I didn't admit it at the time.

When I spoke, in the football stadium, to an audience of over a thousand people, I heard my voice ring out over the microphone and it was as if the energy was moving through me. I could feel the strength of the thought-form but I was separate from it. It was kind of surreal. When I was done, I felt complete, because I had completely given what I wanted to.

Afterwards, I realized that the giving what I had found to be true and giving it completely was enriching to me. I believe this was a defining moment in me knowing that I wanted to be a teacher in some capacity.

Defining moments in adulthood:
*Finding out the difference between ideas and experience. I found an old journal entry where I'd written in giant letters CONCENTRATION AND DISCIPLINE IS THE KEY. I wrote this in the midst of a rambling entry about how to figure out what to do with my life. To this day I don't even remember writing it. It must have come from my subconscious mind, certainly not from my conscious mind or brain. I found the journal entry after I'd been an SOM student for awhile and had been practicing concentration and discipline. I knew that what I had written previously was truth, but when I wrote it I did nothing about it so it was basically worthless at the time.
*When I became a director of an SOM branch, at a Christmas party where we were making decorations for the tree in the school, I realized I was in love with all my students and had a deep insight into what love is. Also realized that I was being for my students the kind of influence that my father had been for me, which was the fulfillment of something in myself I thought had been taken away from me when he died.
*The Angel in the Restaurant story I wrote about in Karmic Healing—admitting that all of my experiences are for soul growth and spiritual progression and to be grateful for what's in my life. Understanding what unconditional giving is and expecting to receive from God when I give to people. (How to transform resentment)

Leaving a Permanent Impression by *Erika Scholz*

I was working as a medical records secretary at a not-for-profit health care agency. On Thursday mornings an older woman named Vera volunteered in my department. She helped with filing patient records. She was a soft, round, pleasant woman whose wrinkles told of many years spent laughing. Her low voice would roll across the room as she told me stories about her grand babies and great grand babies. I would hear stories of her daughter in the military and her son's troubles settling down. I appreciated the time she gave every Thursday and was always thankful for her help.

I decided to leave my job and return to school full-time. On my last Thursday with Vera, she got up to leave. She turned to me and her gentle brown eyes filled with tears. "You don't know how much it's meant to me to come here every week. Before I started volunteering here I felt old and useless. I had a stroke and could no longer do the things I used to do. I thought my time here was done. I was ready to die. Each week I would come here and you always made me feel like my work here was so important to you. Thank you for giving me a reason to live."

With that, she hugged me and walked out of my life, leaving a permanent understanding behind. In that moment I was filled with awe and wonder. I had been given a chance to change someone's life so profoundly and all I had done was shown kindness. I knew in that moment that I had the power to change the world- that was what I was here for. From that day forward, my life would be a journey to bring that to fruition.

Growing Up is Coming Home by *Debbie Dale*

-Good upbringing and love from family

-Growing up with peer pressure, who you really are shines

-Graduating high school and going to college

-Turning 21, wild and crazy college days and nights

-Ages 21-28 very confusing, yet learning years, started interest in crystals and Seth books, knowing there is something more, I just need to find it

-Ages 28-35 having 2 boys totally change my life. I finally needed to learn responsibility. Learning through different relationships with men.

-April, 34 years old. Nervous breakdown. Given grace.

-Age 36, finding the School of Metaphysics. Learning so much-I'm thinking as a soul not just a human here for one chance. I'm less hard on myself and more focused and centered than I have ever been. This is what I've been searching for! It's like finally coming home, a warm fuzzy feeling.

Christ Consciousness in our Lifetime by **Barbara Condron**

Entering School of Metaphysics was a defining moment in my life. At the age of 22 I had completed the kind of education offered by the physical world. I knew I always wanted to learn, all of my life. That's why I had chosen journalism as the major area of concentration at University of Missouri. I imagined I would be able to keep meeting new people, learning new things, every day for the rest of my life and be paid for it. It seemed like the best career I could choose for myself.

By the time I had done the work, made the grades, held the paper, I was lost. Experience in reporting for the city newspaper had taught me this was not how I wanted to spend my life. I fell into a depression, a listless existence of working at temporary jobs, wasted evenings teetotaling with a few friends or alone, dreamless sleep, and then getting up to do it all over again.

Moments of awakening came when one of those friends told me about her Past Life Profile, then shared it with me over dinner a few weeks later. The information, the insight, in this report touched me in a way few things had. I wasn't at all sure about the reincarnation part, yet my natural curiosity had been opened again. The intuitive profile stimulated me to think about the "more" in life. Here the why's were answered.

My friend wanted to go to a class but not alone so I went with her as an act of love, a favor. What I experienced in that three hour class was a defining moment.

I came face to face with my destiny, the reason I am on the planet and the answer to one of my biggest questions, "How can I continue learning?" I find that by passing on what I have learned, particularly truth that is universal, I receive back manifold what I give through helping others. Through giving I ensure my own continued learning.

Almost three decades later a defining moment of another sort came into my life. The focal point surrounded my mother's passing from physical life, the circumstances and aftermath. I had experienced many ego battles through my learning. Some externalized, all internal. I had grown to see these major disrupters of peace as the storm before the calm. I would reference Matthew Chapter 4 from the Bible often as a reminder to be honest with Self's purpose, to be true to my ideals, to practice self respect and emotional control, to learn how to ask questions and listen to my inner self for guidance.

This passage where Satan tempts Jesus with physical powers and delights reached a zenith in my consciousness at this point in my life. At a time when I could have gotten lost in the darkness of hurt, anger, bitterness, regret, abandonment, envy, lust, and other emotional sins, I met the test, choosing to remain in the Light. Although my ego was wounded many times over, I knew I Am and because of that I could meet each temptation for denial, revenge, resentment, blame, and the like.

This was a lesson in love. By identifying the elements of love – acceptance, purpose, compassion, forgiveness, allowing, appreciation, fulfilment, giving, receiving – I stepped into my potential as a whole self.

I learned a great deal about what causes peace through understanding the composition of love. My little ego constantly motivated me, and I chose again and again to live as a Christ with love in my heart and respect in my mind. It was during this time that I consciously embodied, to the full range of my capability, the universal tenet: "love ye one another."

The experience forever changed me. It helped make me who I Am.

What is Friendship
Daniel R. Condron

Connectedness in Love
distilled to one sentence
Friendship is connected in Love.

My experience of receiving
Breath in, Breath out

My experience of giving
Breath out, Breath in

All with an open Heart.

Footnotes from *Lesson Three*

18-19 From Betty Williams acceptance speech upon receipt of the Nobel Peace Prize delivered on Dec. 10, 1977 in Oslo, Norway. © The Nobel Foundation 1977

What is friendship?
John B. Crainshaw

People helping each other fulfill their soul's desires.

<u>Receiving</u>
Before this experience my heart felt broken my mind's energy weak and a burden of entrapment weighed heavy on my shoulders. This experience allowed me to let go of all that and exist in stillness.

<u>Giving</u>
As I gave my awareness expanded into serenity like in meditation.

WHAT IS FRIENDSHIP?
John Harrison

Friendship is sharing your / myself with others and in return unconditionally receiving them. It is when you place the need of another equal to or above your own.

Friendship is becoming one with another person.

It was very interesting to hear other's statements about what friendship is. The one that inspired me the most is "Friendship is fostering truth in each other."
It was fun being bounced around as we moved. It was also fun to see the expressions on people's faces.

Lesson Four

SERVICE

*"A man's life and his dream
can become one"*

He was a well educated son of a Lutheran minister, who received his Nobel Peace Prize for demonstrating "a man's life and his dream can become one" and for turning the concept of brotherhood into living reality.

Albert Schweitzer was born to French parents in the province of Alsace which had until four years before been part of France, and was then, in 1875, a part of Germany. The political locale of this area influenced Schweitzer's life. A many-sided genius, Schweitzer could have followed a career in philosophy, theology, or music – he had doctorates in each. He wrote books on Bach, Jesus, and the German poet, philosopher Goethe. Early on he decided when he reached the age of 30 he would devote the rest of his life to service to humanity.

In 1904, Schweitzer read an article about medical missionaries in the Congo. At age 30 he entered medical school.

Nine years later, he traveled with his newlywed wife, a nurse, to French Equatorial Africa (now Gabon) where they founded a Protestant hospital. His personal philosophy was "reverence for life" which he demonstrated in the way he worked with the people native to this area. His hospital resembled a native village. There was no electricity except in the operating room, animals roamed about and family members lived with their ailing relatives. In Schweitzer's world all people lived together with dignity and responsibility.

In his acceptance speech, Schweitzer said,

"Because the will of the people, being the will of the crowd, has not avoided the danger of instability and the risk of emotional distraction from the path of true reason, it has failed to demonstrate a vital sense of responsibility. Nationalism of the worst sort was displayed in the last two wars, and it may be regarded today as the greatest obstacle to mutual understanding between peoples.

"Such nationalism can be repulsed only through the rebirth of a humanitarian ideal among men which will make their allegiance to their country a natural one inspired by genuine ideals...

"All men, even the semicivilized and the primitive, are, as beings capable of compassion, able to develop a humanitarian spirit. It abides within them like tinder ready to be lit, waiting only for a spark."[20]

Schweitzer was the spark for many. After being closed down and deported to France during the first world war, he returned and by the 1930's his hospital had grown into a complex of 70 buildings staffed by volunteer medical personnel. His ideal of brotherhood and respecting all life was a reality that many shared. When he was given the $33,000 in prize money in 1953, he used it to build a separate facility for lepers.

Schweitzer lived 90 years continuing to perform surgery and give Bach recitals up to the age of 85. The last ten years of his life he was an outspoken opponent of nuclear war, calling for a ban on nuclear weapons.

In his acceptance speech, Schweitzer described what he believed he brought to the world this way:

"I am well aware that what I have had to say on the problem of peace is not essentially new. It is my profound conviction that the solution lies in our rejecting war for an ethical reason; namely, that war makes us guilty of the crime of inhumanity....

"The only originality I claim is that for me this truth goes hand in hand with the intellectual certainty that the human spirit is capable of creating in our time a new mentality, an ethical mentality. Inspired by this certainty, I too proclaim this truth in the hope that my testimony may help to prevent its rejection as an admirable sentiment but a practical impossibility. Many a truth has lain unnoticed for a long time, ignored simply because no one perceived its potential for becoming reality." [21]

One of the most personal of truths that remains unnoticed by many during their lives, is the purpose for their existence. Most people like to think they make a difference, that their life counts, yet few take the time to turn this wishful thinking into conscious living. "Living peaceably begins by thinking peacefully" is the slogan of the Universal Hour of Peace, celebrated around the world as we move from one year to the next.

Thinking peacefully is determined in large measure when you answer the question, "Why am I here?" In part this is answered when you can identify the nature of your learning. Reading, writing, math, and the classic arts and sciences are an attempt to give you the tools you need to elucidate this. Sometimes they do, sometimes they cause confusion rather than clarity, prejudice rather than open-mindedness.

A physical answer can be given for the question "why am I here?" We can believe we are here to be a great composer, manager, or athlete, or maybe we are here to be a good son or daughter or to be at the right place at the right time to save someone's life.

There are also metaphysical answers to the question. There are soul reasons for our lives that warrant investigation. Becoming conscious of these is a key to peace of mind. Composing songs that others enjoy singing and playing is rewarding, yet experiencing the ability to hold your attention on a dozen instruments that exist only in your mind's eye then single out one at a time reflects the reality of your soul's learning. The inner subtleties of learning are permanent understandings in the realm of the soul. It is like being able to remember and interpret your night time dreams. Realizing what we are here to learn inspires Self control, fosters Self discipline, and produces Self awareness.

Another response to "Why am I here?" is the conscious recognition of dharma. Dharma is a Sanskrit word meaning "duty". Dharma is the description of how the soul is full, the configuration the understandings of creation have made. Usually this form can be described in one word, like synthesis, comfort, or integrity. Those attending this day's PeaceMakers are aware of their Dharma either through studying in the SOM course or through participating in a Spiritual Focus Weekend on *Your Soul's Purpose*.

Exploring the Dharma is a wonderful way to experience the reality of Schweitzer's life. His dedication to service, steadfast and compassionate, was an inspiration to the world. It motivated others into action, it comforted others just knowing someone like him existed in the world. Each of us have a purpose, a function to perform in the world. It is beyond our physical, waking consciousness. It is not premeditated or fabricated by the conscious mind. It is the result of lifetimes of experience, like putting the wisdom of all your heroes or favorite writers or world leaders into one soul.

The experience of receiving the intuitive report which helps illuminate your dharma, the Dharma report, is illuminating. Receiving the detailed description of what the duty is, how it came about, and how you can be more aware, more awake in your response to it, is fulfilling, sometimes overwhelming. If you have yet to have this kind of intuitive report, you can begin to grasp your dharma by asking others how they experience you. This is beyond what they think about you (you're pretty, nice, a good friend, etc.) and beyond how they feel about you (good, comfortable, excited, competitive). How you experience someone is what they bring to every interaction, like the universal qualities you will learn about below. Many times people are unaware of their influence. Identifying your dharma changes this. It frees you to be that spark that ignites others, a quality shared by all Nobel Peace Prize winners.

Today's multidimensional experience centered on each person's dharma. To experience our own "ethical mentality" as Schweitzer termed it, we started in a circle. One person would address each present, one after another, by saying the word describing their dharma. Laurie Biswell began by turning to Dr. Pam Blosser and saying, "Magnanimous", to which Dr. Pam replied, "Expansive." Laurie wrote down what she had heard and then proceeded on to the next person, continuing until she had the feedback of everyone present.

Those responding were to describe the first image that came into their minds upon hearing the dharmic word.

The exercise is enriching. It causes the mind to be focused and still even when the attention is not directly related to you, and in that way creates a connectedness of energies with those present, the reality of spiritual brotherhood.

Once everyone received their responses, we used those words to fashion a poem which would serve to help us to develop greater conscious awareness and alignment with our dharmas.

Loyalty

I was born from forever,
with resonant passion faithful to love.
Through connectedness,
I grow an affinity for adhering, for steadfastness.
I am a friend of listening,
and will listen for ever.
–*Paul Madar*

Generosity

To be abundant...
At once there was inclusive eternity
while I was giving kindness and open to fullness
Always connected in selfless receiving and prosperous.
–*Christine Madar*

Justice

The honorable savior has come; let's unify
let's open-mind,
let's rightify;
Riding by; a wave of balance as a wake.
Integrity as a foundation;
let's fortify
Seeing tyranny with a radiant eye;
respectify and rectify.
– *John B. Crainshaw*

Magnanimous

O' Friend
How bountiful is my love for you
your greatness is generous
Expansive and giving in all that you do.
Absorbing, compassion,
pervasive in nature
your generous heart is bountiful for every one.
–*Laurie J. Biswell*

Connectedness

The union of comforting is magnetic to me
The oneness of everyone gives existence of free
The loving of all is the Real I see
The relativity of wholeness will elevate we.
–*Dr. Daniel R. Condron*

S
E
R
V
I
C
E

Productivity

The life adding result,
of energetic creativity.
My action of accomplishment,
brings continuity.
The achievement of Christhood
by all of the people
I resolve to activate my dharma,
bringing light to the world.
–*Erika Scholz*

Faithfulness

Faithfulness is my loving singularity
Continuity brings me to stability
endearing in my loyalty
my devotion is to purity
In emptiness I perceive my expectation
Enlightenment is my dedication.
–*Tad Messenger*

Service

I serve in exhalation
giving freely to all.
My sacred duty is to be attentive to the call
Helping, loving humanity is
my philanthropy
Humanitarianism is fulfillment—
I can be.
–*Mari Hamersley*

Co-operation

Harmony of creation
uplifting unity.
Following, abiding
receptive movement.
Uniting together.
One
–Matthew D. Marian

Attending

Being with.
Concentrated patience.
Being devoted to the present
brings a gracious connectedness
that supports and brings ease in the moment.
–Dr. Pam Blosser

Warmth

Sunshine is melting all of my cool
Outpouring healing energy into my room.
Enlightening my life with genuine living
The comfort I seek is everywhere giving.
–John Harrison

Elevation

I raise my eyes from whence I came
wondering how I might regain
the heights from which epiphany comes
and inspiration freely runs.

"How can I soar? What will uplift?"
the cry of joy leaves my fingertips.
"By character," I hear the voice.
"Expand me," replies my choice.

"The secret to enlighten is within
come join with me to ascend."
I lift my hand to touch the sun
In Shiva's mind compassion's won.

–Dr. Barbara Condron

The responsibility lies with each of us to fulfill our part of a much greater whole. Doing so is knowing and living your dharma. The refrain of recent years, "Think globally, act locally," takes on real meaning in the light of how Albert Schweitzer conducted his thoughts and actions. Schweitzer himself aptly noted, *"Only when an ideal of peace is born in the minds of the peoples will the institutions set up to maintain this peace effectively fulfill the function expected of them."*

In 1973, the School of Metaphysics was formed as an institution of higher learning, devoted to the acceleration of evolution through aiding any individual to become a whole, functioning self. The means to accomplish Schweitzer's ideas exists. SOM affords the means for people to create ideals and use their minds more fully, more productively, through the practice of concentration and meditation, and the development of reasoning and intuition.

From this ideal came a description of peace unparalled in the history of our world – the *Universal Peace Covenant*. This detailed description of peace was created from October to April 1997. It is the result of the spiritual collaboration of people from all walks of life, several religious beliefs and nationalities, diverse occupations, all races, as young as seventeen and as old as seventy-five. What we had in common was we were all teachers in the School of Metaphysics.

Over nine months, we came together with the intention of creating a timeless document that would accurately reflect humanity's hope, challenge, and destiny.

The result is ...

The Universal Peace Covenant

Peace is the breath of our spirit.
It wells up from within the depths of our being to refresh, to heal, to inspire.

Peace is our birthright.
Its eternal presence exists within us as a memory of where we have come from and as a vision of where we yearn to go.

Our world is in the midst of change.
For millennia, we have contemplated, reasoned, and practiced the idea of peace. Yet the capacity to sustain peace eludes us. To transcend the limits of our own thinking we must acknowledge that peace is more than the cessation of conflict. For peace to move across the face of the earth we must realize, as the great philosophers and leaders before us, that all people desire peace. We hereby acknowledge this truth that is universal. Now humanity must desire those things that make for peace.

We affirm that peace is an idea whose time has come.
We call upon humanity to stand united, responding to the need for peace. We call upon each individual to create and foster a personal vision for peace. We call upon each family to generate and nurture peace within the home. We call upon each nation to encourage and support peace among its citizens. We call upon each leader, be they in the private home, house of worship or place of labor, to be a living example of peace for only in this way can we expect peace to move across the face of the earth.

World Peace begins within ourselves.
Arising from the spirit peace seeks expression through the mind, heart, and body of each individual. Government and laws cannot heal the heart. We must transcend whatever separates us. Through giving love and respect, dignity and comfort, we come to know peace. We learn to love our neighbors as we love ourselves bringing peace into the world. We hereby commit ourselves to this noble endeavor.

Peace is first a state of mind.
Peace affords the greatest opportunity for growth and learning which

leads to personal happiness. Self-direction promotes inner peace and therefore leads to outer peace. We vow to heal ourselves through forgiveness, gratitude, and prayer. We commit to causing each and every day to be a fulfillment of our potential, both human and divine.

Peace is active, the motion of silence, of faith, of accord, of service. It is not made in documents but in the minds and hearts of men and women. Peace is built through communication. The open exchange of ideas is necessary for discovery, for well-being, for growth, for progress whether within one person or among many. We vow to speak with sagacity, listen with equanimity, both free of prejudice, thus we will come to know that peace is liberty in tranquility.

Peace is achieved by those who fulfill their part of a greater plan. Peace and security are attained by those societies where the individuals work closely to serve the common good of the whole. Peaceful coexistence between nations is the reflection of man's inner tranquility magnified. Enlightened service to our fellowman brings peace to the one serving, and to the one receiving. We vow to live in peace by embracing truths that apply to us all.

Living peaceably begins by thinking peacefully.
We stand on the threshold of peace-filled understanding. We come together, all of humanity, young and old of all cultures from all nations. We vow to stand together as citizens of the Earth knowing that every question has an answer, every issue a resolution. As we stand, united in common purpose, we hereby commit ourselves in thought and action so we might know the power of peace in our lifetimes.

Peace be with us all ways. May Peace Prevail On Earth.

signed this 8th day of October, 1997, at the College of Metaphysics

Dr. Barbara Condron   Dr. Daniel Condron   Dr. Pam Blosser   Dr. Sheila Benjamin

Dr. Laurel Clark   Dr. Al Rohrer   Paul Blosser   Melanie McManus   Linda Yeingst   Ernie Padilla

Teresa Padilla   Terry Martin   Christine Andrews   Sharka Glet   Jay McCormick   Greg Hoeflicker

Lisa Kinser   John Clark   Patrick Andries   Damian Nordmann   Mari Hamersley   Terryll Nemeth

Paul Madar   Oliver Seger   Lyle Branson   John Harrison   Traci Byington   Shannon Cordes

My spirit soars every time I read the *Covenant*. Through the years I have come to respect its majesty. Few historical documents I have read resonate with its brilliance. The Constitution of the United States is one. As that document lit a light so all the world could see that people can live together with freedom, I am certain the *Universal Peace Covenant* will influence the spirit of the world for good in the centuries to come.

What is Friendship
Greg Brown

It is one who can aid another when needed,
one who can listen and teach one to fish when needed.
Friendship to me is the essence of unconditional love and giving
for the goodness of all concerned. Friendship is a soul to soul, spirit to spirit
connection — that is timeless. It is beyond the conscious mind.

It is **a soul bond that is timeless and ageless**
with the foundation of unconditional love and giving.

My experience of giving was fulfilling.
I gave from my heart with ease.

Receiving was fulfilling.
I received into my heart with ease:
Much Love to give and Receive.

Footnote from *Lesson Four*

20-22 From Albert Schweitzer's speech upon receipt of the Nobel Peace Prize entitled "The Problem of Peace" delivered on November 4, 1954 in Oslo. © The Nobel Foundation, 1954.

What is Friendship?
Chris Sheehan

Friendship is
- cooperation in creation - love - compatibility between souls
- avenue or vehicle for the expression of love
- the experience is a mutually beneficial relationship between people

**A mutually beneficial loving relationship between people
for learning and growth.**

giving — my experience of giving was valuable. I felt connected with
everyone in the other circle. Also the group of us on the inner circle
were all speaking in unison however we were all diverse in our description
of the one. It felt powerful to be a part of the whole giving to this
other half.

receiving — All the expressions were correct
and they all stated the same essence.
It was a self respect moment to experience that.

Mandy Boland

Friendship is . . . .Sharing
Loving because of and inspite of differences and similarities
Caring. Giving your best. Looking over, moving past the bad spots.
Forgiving   Respect   Connecting   Harmonizing.   Trust.

When giving to a friend as you would like to receive.
Friends work through all snags & keep Loving.

I felt an incredible connection with each person 1st receiving from them
without hesitation and then giving on both the in breath and out
and with my all. A great amount of emotion.

Trust in each to receive and give.

Linda Yeingst

Thought — Friendship is the universal bond
of Divine Love which combines
the laws of Infinity and Relativity.

In Receiving —
I felt a tingle of energy move up my spine as I received the
truth and love offered by the other person completely. We
become one for a moment. I felt tears of love and joy
coming from within.

In Giving —
I focused totally on my thought — projecting it with love
and friendship.

Sebastian Hartman

Friendship is a perfect circle of love.
The circle is always able to expand to take on something new.
This openness is present on all ends because you must be filled
with love and connection to see what is best
and you must be open to receive.

**Friendship is an ever-expanding connection built on universal love,
proper perspective, and growth.**

As I was receiving
I recognized the unity of thought that was present.
It was a deeply connecting experience.

My experience of giving was equally amazing
because I was able to connect with the image more and more
as I went on, and with the beautiful people.

PEACEMAKING PEACEMAKING PEACEMAKING PEACEMAKING

Lesson Five

INTELLIGENCE

*"We, you and I,
              are privileged to be alive
        during this extraordinary age..."*

"We, you and I, are privileged to be alive during this extraordinary age, this unique epoch in the history of the world, the epoch of demarcation between the past millennia of war and suffering, and the future, the great future of peace, justice, morality, and human well-being."[23]

These words were spoken in 1962 when scientist Linus Pauling accepted his second Nobel, this one for Peace.

Eight years earlier Pauling was awarded the Nobel Prize in his field, chemistry, for his long-time investigation of the forces that hold molecules together in matter. It is Pauling who developed the resonance theory to explain molecular bonding, and his studies led to his discovery of the atomic structure of protein molecules which opened the door to understanding the chemistry of the human body and its diseases.

By this time, Pauling's interest in human chemistry had led him to begin investigating the effects on the body of radioactive fallout, particles and gases that are the by-products of exploding nuclear weapons. He was convinced that increasing amounts of fallout in the world — the consequences of atomic bomb blasts and nuclear testing, beginning in the 1940s — had become a major cause of certain types of disease as well as mental retardation and physical deformity. Alarmed, he began a vigorous crusade against nuclear weapons testing.

By 1962, this Portland, Oregon native who was not allowed to graduate from high school yet earned Bachelor's degrees in chemistry and physics, and later received a doctorate from CalTech, displayed the genius characteristic of those who see beyond what exists into tomorrow. His steadfastness contributed to the partial nuclear test ban treaty of 1963 between the U.S., Great Britain, and the Soviet Union. Pauling had drafted a proposal that served as the basis of the test ban treaty.

Although Pauling remained committed to world peace and disarmament, he devoted most of the remainder of his life to scientific research. His research into the curative powers of vitamins, particularly vitamin C, he called orthomolecular medicine. As with Schweitzer, Pauling's natal environmental influence showed in his work. His father was a pharmacist. His books on the subject were best sellers: *Cancer and Vitamin C* and *How to Live Longer and Feel Better*.

A living example of what he believed, Pauling lived to the age of 93. His was a full life contributing to the betterment of mankind and that which he valued the most. The fact is, to date he is the only individual who has received separate Nobel Prizes in both a scientific and a nonscientific field.

Pauling had a clear vision of what could be. He knew how privileged mankind is to have the opportunity "of contributing to the achievement of the goal of the abolition of war and its replacement by world law." He said he was confident that we would succeed in meeting this challenge.

Pauling saw a world often enslaved by its own limitations. Being a reasoner, he could see the alternatives. Like many Peace Prize winners before him, he knew there were alternatives to the war and the suffering it causes. The answer would require people to think in new ways.

"...through the better use of the earth's resources, of the discoveries of scientists, and of the efforts of mankind, from hunger, disease, illiteracy, and fear; and that we shall in the course of time be enabled to build a world characterized by economic, political, and social justice for all human beings and a culture worthy of man's intelligence." [24]

Pauling's words – "a culture worthy of man's intelligence" – linger, inviting further reflection. In six well-chosen and well-placed words Pauling offers inspiration and challenge. The implication is we can do more. We can do better.

Who are we as a culture? What and who do we celebrate? Where do we place our values? Many great masters have taught that where you place your value, you will also find your heart. Whether that heart swells with pride or breaks with sorrow depends largely upon what happens in your head.

Considering man's intelligence makes us think more deeply about ourselves. Linus Pauling believed in man's inherent intelligence. He saw evidence of man's ability to create, and his experience told him that this creativity could be directed toward solving the problems of humankind.

Pauling knew, as did other Nobel Prize laureates, that we have created many of these problems ourselves. He placed much of the responsibility on the shoulders of his peers – fellow scientists. This also told him that we have within our means solutions.

"The world has been greatly changed, especially during the last century, by the discoveries of scientists. Our increased knowledge now provides the possibility of eliminating poverty and starvation, of decreasing significantly the suffering caused by disease, of using the resources of the world effectively for the benefit of humanity." [25]

It was the discoveries of scientists also led to the splitting of the atom and subsequent developments toward weapons of mass destruction. Pauling did not shy away from the truth. Science had unleashed these powers upon the world – like Pandora's curiosity loosing all manner of pain upon mankind – and it would be up to scientists to develop what is needed to respond to those powers with wisdom.

"But the greatest of all the changes has been in the nature of war, the several million-fold increase in the power of explosives, and corresponding changes and methods of delivery of bombs.

"These changes have resulted from the discoveries of scientists, and during the last two decades scientists have taken a leading part in bringing them to the attention of their fellow human beings and in urging that vigorous action be taken to prevent the use of the new weapons and to abolish war from the world." [26]

Pauling had faith in man's intelligence. A sense of destiny and the capacity to meet it were evident in his writings and his speeches. His faith was not so much religious as it was spiritual. He appealed to common sense, to the reasoner in each of us, while respecting the inner Self, the spirit.

"Our political leaders impelled by the massed feelings of the people of the world must learn that peace is the important goal – a peace that reflects the spirit of true humanity, the spirit of the brotherhood of man."

Many hear the word peace without ever experiencing its fullness. One believes peace will come only at death. Another defines it as the absence of war. Another says it is a lofty concept not meant to be obtained by mortals in this world. Such people are in need of a vital element of reasoning – imagination!

Outstanding people in all fields – from science to the arts – display four essential living skills: the ability to give attention at will, memory recall, imagination, and listening. Our exercise this morning was an opportunity to use them all. In the spirit of Linus Pauling, we explored peace from a reasoner's point of view. Employing whatever we have learned about the nature of man's intelligence, we identified what produces peace and, in true scientific fashion, we created equations describing it.

What we came up with is, once again, enlightening, hopeful, thought-provoking and a great deal of fun.

Peace Equations

sparked by Linus Pauling

(World plus Man) minus (war plus death) multiplied by (love times infinity) to the power of infinity. This divided by (the world plus Man) minus (war plus death) equals peace (the sun with a man's face, the thinker, radiating Light). To simplify the equation, cancel out the similar parts of the equations on the top and bottom and what you are left with is (love times infinity) raised to infinity equals peace. **–John Crainshaw**

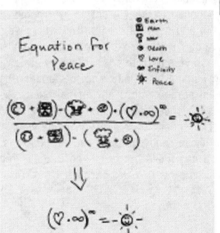

Three equations, because it keeps getting more complex. The first one is a triangle: one plus one equals one. To explain that: take the differences in the past (n-3) plus the differences in the present (c-2) plus all the differences in the future (m-1), and divide by all the aspects of Self (144,000) and multiply by infinite relationship of all the souls on earth, which equals "We are all One". n=negroid, c=caucasoid, m=mongoloid **–Tad Messenger**

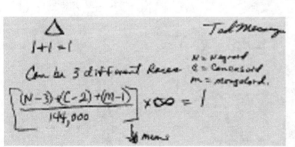

Person giving love, plus a person receiving love, raised to the nth power, where n equals all the people that give and receive love, which equals peace. Another equation is Love times People, times Stillness and Giving, equals the World receiving Peace. **–Matthew Marian**

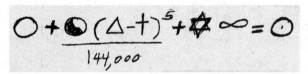

The equation begins with a whole that is complete and in infancy, neither either, yet both. This is added to the aggressive and receptive factors of creation as they manifest through you personally, symbolized by yin-yang symbol. This is multiplied by creation (the triangle) minus limitation (the cross), then this number is multiplied to the 5th power (reasoning). Dividing by 144,000 aspects creates the whole self. This sum is added to the six-pointed star which symbolizes the Universal Truth "As Above so Below." This is now multiplied by Infinity, and that equals the same little round person with a dot in the middle, which is the still and concentrated mind – I AM He – which is Peace. The geometric form is the circle with the pentagon in it over and over, connected, which is an infinity. You can move out or in and it keeps repeating itself over and over. **–Dr. Barbara Condron**

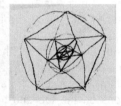

Truth (t and the sun) multiplied by Forgiveness (f and hands praying) and Gratitude (g and smiling face), raised to the power of Love (heart), equals peace (peace symbol of dove print). **–Erika Scholz**

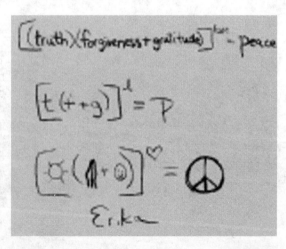

$$(C + U - I)(M + R - F)(G + S + D - G)(W) = P$$

$$\left[\left(\frac{I}{C+U}\right)\left(\frac{F}{M+R}\right)\left(\frac{G}{G+S+D}\right)(W)\right]^{\infty} = ?$$

Pam Blosser

Curiosity (C) plus Desire for Understanding (U) minus Ignorance (I), times Mental Concern (M) plus Respect (R) minus Fear (F), times Goodness for all concerned (G) plus Soul Growth (S) plus Spiritual Development (D) minus Greed times Will (W) to make it happen, equals Peace (P) **–Dr. Pam Blosser**

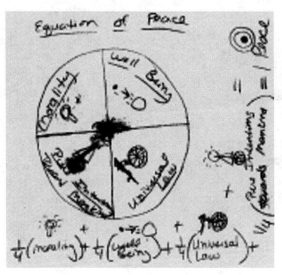

1/4 Morality (mirror) plus 1/4 Well-being (a dot effecting the whole O) plus 1/4 Universal Law (staff/snake effecting the wheel of karma) plus 1/4 Pure intentions for mankind (superconscious sun over mind triangle with singular ideal and purpose vertical line influencing the earth below) equals 1, which is peace (concentric rings around dot). All done in the shape of a peace pie chart.
–Teresa Padilla

Understanding (A) times Love (B) minus Fear (C) plus Respect (X) times Communication (Y), divided by Equality (Z), equals peace.
–Larry Hudson

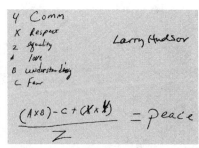

Y Comm
X Respect
Z equality
A love
B understanding
C Fear

Larry Hudson

$$\frac{(A \times B) - C + (X \times Y)}{Z} = peace$$

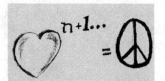

Love, constantly increasing (n+1) to infinity equals peace.
–Paul Blosser

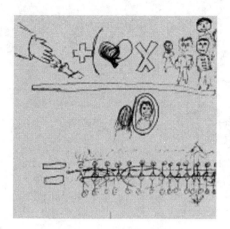

The Heart has aggressive and receptive qualities of love, multiplied by people of different races and backgrounds (five of them to signify reasoning) added to Caring (larger hand helping smaller hand). This is then divided by Self Respect (person looking in mirror), and it all equals peace (people holding hands in a Circle of Love with still minds). –**Laurie Biswell**

$$cM + SM + SCM = P$$

$$G + O + D$$

$$L + O + V + E = P$$

Three equations. Conscious Mind plus Subconscious Mind plus Superconscious Mind all in alignment equals peace. Also, L+O+V+E = Peace, and G+O+D is peace. –**John Harrison**

$$\frac{(*)(\leftrightarrow)}{O \times 7 \times \bar{\alpha}} + \phi \times \odot \xrightarrow{\Omega} \left[\sum_{\bigtriangledown}^{\Delta \to \infty} \right.$$

Where are we and where do we want to be? Starting in a world situation (according to Linus Pauling) of Fear, Self-consumption and avoidance (*) multiplied by separateness (<->). As you divide that situation (interrupt that pattern) with experience of Oneness (O) multiplied by Universal Law (7) and Wisdom (a), and then add Self Respect (faces in mirror) and multiply by present mindedness (circle with dot), it leads to the continual expansion (summation) of love given (heart expands) and therefore continual change of consciousness (triangle to infinity). –**Paul Madar**

Two equations. Love (heart) plus Connectedness (people holding hands) equals peace (dove). Connectedness is Ultimate Truth, so Love plus Truth equals Peace (Light). Other equation is Stillness (S) plus Openness (O) equals Peace (P). Simple when you use the Mind correctly. Healing requires effort: choice, practice, will, effort. **–Dr. Daniel Condron**

$$S + O = P$$

While the adults were creating their formulas, Daniel's and my 8-year-old son circled the group in Indigo fashion. After a while, he came into the center, grabbed a piece of paper and some pencils and moved close to one of the people on my right. I began working on my equation.

Within minutes he had moved to face me. He was looking into my face, while I was talking to Laurie. Undeterred, he came within inches mentally insisting that I look at him, which I did. His big bright eyes looked into mine and he said, "I need to see your eyes!" I smiled, and he pulled back and started writing something.

He made his way around the circle in the following ten minutes and came over between Dan and I, showing us what he had done. On the paper were horizontal lines, each about an inch and a half long, in a vertical column stretching from the top of the page to the bottom. I looked at Ki with questioning eyes.

"It's the color of everyone's eyes."

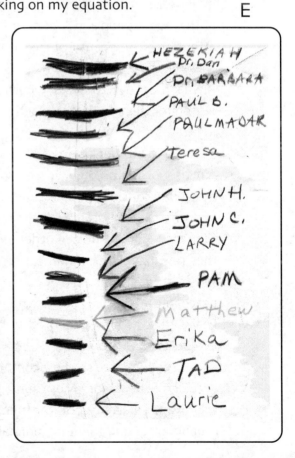

"Really, Hezekiah?" I was amazed. "That's what you've been doing?"

He nodded, a shy smile curving his lips. "Do you like it?"

"I think it's wonderful Ki. What made you think of this?"

He shrugged as if he didn't know what to say. I could appreciate the inner, subconscious connection Ki had with all of us present. What a wonderful lesson. How looking into someone's eye you see the Real Self. What it requires to be able to look someone in the eye, and what it can give back to you.

Since talk of nuclear war had been a part of this circle, and an increasing reality in our global lives, memory of a TV movie I had seen years ago, probably around 1970, called the *World War III* surfaced in my consciousness. The image of the ending of the movie was very clear, and very relevant to today's train of thought.

The movie tells the tale of what could happen if the (then) two major superpowers allowed hot heads to overcome cold hearts, something both Linus Pauling and Albert Schweitzer repeatedly brought to everyone's attention. The beauty of the story, and the reason it stayed with me all these years, is the way it ends. Two men, one from the U.S. and one from Russia, meet eye-to-eye and in that moment they realize there is no good reason for them to destroy each other. The concept brings a deeper meaning to seeing eye-to-eye.

The moment is an epiphany for these two characters. Without benefit of words, for they do not speak the same language, they come to newfound conclusions about each other. They realize they need each other, and whatever differences they may have believed separated them enough that they would kill each other over them, disappear in the light of what they now have in common.

It was Mohandas K. Gandhi, probably the greatest proponent of peace in the 20th century – who incidentally was never awarded a Nobel Peace Prize – who was quoted as saying that *"the only thing 'an eye for an eye' succeeds in doing is making a world full of blind people."*

Children are the best common motivation humans have for ceasing destructive behavior. Most humans want the best for their offspring, and they want a better world for them to inherit. Love is the great incentive capable of taking material, animal man and transforming him into spiritual, intuitive man.

In order to produce a quantum leap in evolution, we must become reasoners. Pauling was a reasoner, as were Schweitzer, King, Williams, and Mother Teresa. When the thoughts change, the actions follow suit.

My son's innovative peace project also caused me to remember a woman (her name eludes me) I saw on television years ago. She was an elementary schoolteacher. In her classroom there came a time each year when she divided the class into "the blue eyes" and "the brown eyes." Within a few days she began to treat them differently, the blue eyes were inferior, not quite as smart or wealthy or attractive while the brown eyes were given preferential treatment and dispensations.

Quickly, within a few days, the children began assuming the new identity, treating each other according to assumptions that had been made. It was an amazing exercise in prejudice, what it is and how it is created. The cause was not in the color of the eyes, it was in the beliefs, the thoughts of the children themselves!

This teacher successfully isolated the cause of all prejudice, and the children got to experience the effects. A life lesson, well taught and well learned.

Peace begins in the hearts and minds of men and women. The counsel to love one another is a rich one. It appeals to the head, making good sense. Loving others as we love ourselves makes room in the heart for others to help us fulfill our desires. Certainly all the important lessons in life resolve around this magnetic power that unites souls.

It is the ability to entrain head and heart, to reason and to intuit, that gives us the inner authority and control that brings peace of mind. The ancient edict "know thyself" has endured through the ages for good reason. When we know ourselves, we are more generous with others. As the Universal Peace Covenant states, "Self-direction promotes inner peace and therefore leads to outer peace." Even in an elementary classroom where children find the rules have changed, those who are self-directed, who have an internal compass pointing to Truth that is universal, find a way to hold onto that Truth.

Hezekiah will someday know this story, but for now he is evolving his intelligent brilliance by growing a heart big enough to direct it, and that is changing the way he sees our world.

What is Friendship
Tad Messenger

describes the connection
that already exists between us and others.
We discover it & build friendship through creating together;
cooperating; envisioning; including; interacting; and loving.

Friendship is the divine connection that we all have with others
because we all have the same inner urge.

**Friendship is the Divine Connection that already exists between
individuals.**

Experience of <u>receiving</u>
I sure have a lot of friends
India, other worlds, Atlantis, forever
Talina was a master or guru in India
Ara — Peladean, Dory — Buddhist monk

<u>Giving</u>
Connection with Love
We are all one.
bring forth the Sun
breathe
I and He are one
Friendship is a uniting force.

Footnotes from *Lesson Five*

23-26   Linus Pauling's acceptance speech entitled
"Science and Peace" delivered upon receipt of the Nobel
Peace Prize, December 11, 1963 in Oslo, Norway.
© The Nobel Foundation, 1963

What is Friendship?

Resonance
of common ancestry, of similar circumstances,
of dreams and goals — of destiny.

Resonance
of Life moving in the same direction of the fulfillment of
Creator's Plan.

**Friendship is seeing another's soul with your own soul's eyes.
–Paul Madar**

What is Friendship?
Laurel Clark

Friendship is the universal mental attraction that
unites individuals in bonds of divine love. Friendship is meeting
another soul and resonating heart to heart. It is creating together,
sharing dreams and ideals. Friendship is being a companion, holding
someone in your mind and arms and love. It is walking together toward
a common goal. Friendship is acceptance and compassion. Friendship is
delighting in another's growth.
Friendship is learning to love in all of its many expressions and manifestations.
Friendship is soul resonance.

The experience of receiving was delightful. I felt a profound connection and
openness. I allowed the energy of love and friendship to move through me.
I was aware of the temptation to try to control or manage it because
it was so powerful. That really would have meant restricting it. Instead I
allowed it to be and let it move me inward.
Giving was very powerful. Some people seemed bowled over
by what I said, even physically moving backward. I became
aware of a clear truth that grew more clear every time
I said it. I received nourishment of union
with other minds and souls. It was like a cycle —
I gave and received as I was giving
like the truth came into
my soul as I gave it.

Kristy Cannon

Friendship is . . .
~ honest and open communication
~ mental love and respect
~ compassion

Receiving from Everyone was an amazing glimpse into each
person's way of thinking for just a moment.

Giving helps me to remember that I have much
to offer others and see its value.

What is Friendship?
Dory Wheatley

Friendship is crucial to life. It is the outer manifestation
of the inner connectedness. Without Friendship there
can be no expansion. We need each other, to mirror each other,
to give and receive through in order to Know Self and love all of Self.
Every friend is invaluable. All Friends are best Friends. For me
with friends there exists a bond of love that transcends all time and space.
I would do anything to help a friend. We are there for each other.
Shared experiences give us a place for our hearts and minds
to merge and friendship to deepen.
Friendship is a living pulse of love and creation, it nurtures the true Self
and transcends all time and space.
My experience of giving and receiving was one of gratitude, merging with
each soul in friendship. I was very moved from my heart. All was true,
was pure, was the beauty of the real Self.
In giving I practiced giving completely and pouring love and
acceptance into my friend. In receiving I practiced
absorbing the thought given into my whole mind —
the picture — and receiving them — their essence
and their love into my soul.

Lesson Six

VALUE

"Ancient values

that have sustained mankind
are today reaffirming themselves..."

Today's PeaceMaker gathering was held in the ground level of the Peace Dome. The Peace Dome is still under construction and today will be the day we open it to the world by cutting the airform exposing the elliptical opening to the first floor that extends into the top of the dome.

Today we consider the life and words of Tenzin Gyatso, the 14th Dalai Lama of Tibet. Tenzin Gyatso was born July 6, 1935. When he was two, a group of monks identified him as the fourteenth Dalai Lama, the reincarnation of the succession of Tibetan leaders. Dalai means ocean and lama means monk.

It was three years before he took the throne. The region surrounding Tenzin's home was controlled by the Chinese government who demanded payment to let the boy go. One of five children, his parents were peasants. Once seated in Tibet, Tenzin was privately tutored by the monks in preparation for being the spiritual and political leader of Tibet.

In 1950, troops from the newly established communist China invaded Tibet. China declared Tibet a province but allowed it to keep its religious and political system. Small wars broke out. Being opposed to violence in any form, the Dalai Lama refused to take sides.

In 1959, the growing militancy of the occupying Chinese led to a Tibetan rebellion where thousands were killed. The Dalai Lama fled to Dharamsala, India, near Pakistan, with his mother and a sister. The Chinese imposed a communist government on Tibet, killing monks, destroying monasteries and artwork.

For years the Dalai Lama could not travel outside of India because the government didn't want to offend the Chinese. Even so, he was able to help 80,000 Tibetan immigrants and wrote his autobiography.

The travel ban was lifted in 1967 and he was allowed to travel to Japan. Six years later he journeyed to Europe.

By 1979 the Chinese, who had allowed Tibetan monasteries to reopen, invited the Dalai Lama to return. Instead, Tenzin elected to continue traveling abroad in Moscow and the U.S., speaking at colleges stressing the need to end violence. His commitment now was to world peace, and he realized he could do more in exile. As a result, he has been named an honorary citizen of many nations, including the United States.

In 1989 Tenzin Gyatso was awarded the Nobel Peace Prize for his "opposition to violence." Those of us who have met him describe his merit in different ways.

Dr. Laurel Clark was one of five journalists chosen to interview his holiness in St. Louis in 1993. "He is very humble. I have seen him speak at the Parliament of the World's Religions and on film. The Dalai Lama always has a respect for who he is and his relationship with the whole of creation. Even after all that has happened to him, there is a joy that bubbles up from within him that is very delightful and joyful."

Tenzin is an amazing person. When you study his life, it is a normal inclination to conclude if anybody deserves to hold an ounce of bitterness or anger or even self-righteousness, it is this man. Yet when you read his words, when you are in his presence, such human weaknesses are not there.

He is an amazing testimony to what it means to be present, to embody spirituality, to be spiritual man. I look at Tenzin as an example of where I want to go. I want the radiance, ever-present, regardless of situation or circumstance, that emanates from the still mind.

Although Matthew has yet to meet his holiness, he has read his books and interviews with him. "(The writings) remind me of the combination between Dr. Dan and Hezekiah. He has that quality of turning people's heads – really bringing people's attention to where he is. He cracks simple jokes, and has developed a really good sense of humor. It reminds me of that part in the *Bible*– when you can become like children you can enter the kingdom of God."

Having lived in the Orient some years ago, Dr. Pam commented on the Dalai Lama's love for his oppressors. "He loves the Chinese. That to me is amazing. He has talked about how he has this plan where the Chinese can have what they want and the Tibetans can have what they want. He doesn't fight the Chinese. There is just a fountain of giving."

"I also saw him at the World's Parliament of Religions," added Sharka Glet. "I experienced the humbleness too. Everybody was waiting for him to arrive. There were really big spiritual leaders from different religions and they were sitting there proud. This little man comes in and bows to everybody."

I think the first thing that I learned from the Dalai Lama was the reality of infancy in wisdom, how similar infancy (the initial phase of a cycle) and wisdom (the concluding phase of a cycle) are. Part of it comes from a recognition that when you are experiencing the wisdom part of a cycle you are preparing to enter infancy again. The other part is recognizing that in every cycle there are other cycles, the microcosm in the macro-cosm idea.

For instance, when you are in wisdom you smile and laugh a lot. Think of the joy of learning that is alive in a favorite teacher. My choral teacher in high school was such a person. His name was Gordon Beaver and we relentlessly teased him about his name. Apart from his sizable quali-fications to teach 100 teenagers at a time, he was always joyful. I remem-ber his smiling face to this very day, and I remember the songs he placed in my heart.

Think of the endless patience of a grandparent. Where mothers will panic and dads over-react, grandparents take experiences in stride. As a child, whenever I was figuring something out, I would go to my grand-mother. She knew how to give me space to do it myself no matter what "it" might be. There's a lot of freedom in the knowing that wisdom brings.

These kinds of teachers and grandparents delight in their pupil's progress, looking forward to each step with knowing and compassion. The student's pride in accomplishment is their own, so they smile! They are with you and for you all ways.

Tenzin exudes this same sense. With his generous smile and fre-quent giggles, he embodies wisdom to me. Being in his presence gave me permission to be a child, to be free, to be open, to relish innocence and optimism and all the things of infancy. I felt a sense of joy-filled peace that I had left behind years before. I didn't even know it was missing until Tenzin brought it back to me.

I thought deeply about my first experience with the Dalai Lama. In time I realized I had lost this open trust through public schooling which taught me articifical means of maturity. In today's world, too early souls learn they do not want to be children. They develop a desire to disavow their innocence. This prejudice is one of the major problems students in the School of Metpahysics face in their quest for Self realization and it is one of the most severe thieves of peace.

Prejudices retarding growth must be faced and dissolved for spiri-tual progress to take place. As we progress in our journey, we wash the darkness of limitation from our brains and open the intelligently creative potential of the mind to encompass all Truth. Consider these words from the Dalai Lama's speech upon acceptance of the Peace Prize.

"I feel honored, humbled and deeply moved that you should give this important prize to a simple monk from Tibet. I am no one special, but I believe the prize is a recognition of the true value of all truism, laws, compassion and non-violence, which I try to practice in accordance of the teaching of the Buddha and the great sages of India and Tibet." [27]

Always his awareness encompasses more than himself. Practicing Buddhism, the Dalai Lama has adopted a scientific approach to understanding the self. Therefore, it was natural to follow our study of Linus Pauling with His Holiness. Consider the following:

"The problems we face today, violent conflicts, destruction of nature, poverty, hunger and so on are human created problems, which can be resolved through human effort, understanding and the development of a sense of brotherhood and sisterhood. We need to cultivate a universal responsibility for one another and the planet we share. Although I have found my own Buddhist religion helpful in creating love and compassion, even for those we consider our enemies, I am convinced that everyone can develop a good heart and sense of Universal responsibility with or without religion." [28]

This idea was very important for him to articulate. It is generous and omniscient in its scope. Inclusive and accepting in its practice. His concept of Universal responsibility reminds me of the now frequently seen lists of statements from the world's religions which support the Golden Rule; *"Love ye one another."* This Universal Truth is present in some form in all the world's Holy Scriptures.

This quote prompted me to think about the existence of the School of Metaphysics as a place open to all thinkers, of all religions and cultures and backgrounds. To know the Self people must be free to experiment, to experience truth for themselves.

In Linus's speeches there was no mention of religion or God. Nor was there much about brotherhood. His idea centered around decency and ethical morality. These are nonreligious words describing the same core thought, eternal truths that apply to us all. At the School of Metaphysics we can meet, converse, and interact with those of any background in an atmosphere created by the practice of respect.

It is this element of respect that the Dalai Lama spoke so well to during his acceptance speech for the 1989 Nobel Peace Prize. His words reflect his compassionate heart.

"Peace in the sense of the absence of war is of little value for one who is dying of hunger and cold. It will not remove the pain of torture inflicted on a prisoner of conscience. It does not comfort those who have lost loved ones in floods caused by senseless deforestation in a neighboring country. Peace can only last where people's life are respected, where people are fed and when individuals and nations are free.

"Peace starts within each of us. When we have inner peace we can be at peace with those around us. When our community is in a state of peace we can share that peace with neighboring communities and so on and feel love and kindness towards others. It not only makes others feel loved and cared for but it helps us also to develop inner happiness. As a Buddhist monk, my concern extends to all members of the human family and, indeed, to all sentient beings who suffer. I believe all suffering is caused by ignorance. People inflict pain on others in the selfish pursuit of their happiness or satisfaction. Yet true happiness comes from a sense of inner peace and contentment, which in turn must be achieved through the culti- vation of altruism, of love and compassion and elimination of ignorance, selfishness and greed.

"I believe all religions pursue the same goals, that of cultivating human goodness and bringing happiness to all human beings. Though the means might appear different, the ends are the same. As we enter the final decade of this century, I am optimistic that the ancient values that have sustained mankind are today reaffirming themselves to prepare us for a kinder, happier twenty-first century." [29]

Ancient values. Since metaphysics is the exploration of the Univer- sal principles – laws and truths – that govern our existence, it seemed fit- ting that we would contemplate the meaning of the Dalai Lama's words. Our peacemaking exercise this day was to focused our minds for the pur- pose of discerning what these ancient values might be. For fifteen minutes we pondered what values have stood the test of time. How far back can we go? What has caused mankind to exist, progress, to evolve?

When the question first arose in my mind, thoughts of the founders of the United States surfaced and so I wrote about them. "Peace, liberty, and the pursuit of happiness" is how Thomas Jefferson described it. In so many of the thoughts of these great thinkers are the ancient values that sustain mankind. Their vision to establish a government of the people, by the people, and for the people, was a testimony to their faith in humanity to use reasoning. Their ideas reflect appreciation of the human potential to be divine – to become like our Creator.

Next, I asked each person to synthesize their thoughts into a single word that would describe an ancient value.

Here is what I wrote, "The tree of life, universal symbol in every culture on the planet from the Garden of Eden to Asgard to the baobab, came into my mind. Immortality is certainly an ancient value. From the Atlanteans to the Greeks to modern scientists, the yearning for longevity has made immortality highly prized.

"To be made in the image and after the likeness of our Creator, is to have the capacity to know Self. The ancient value is to ask the four pro-found questions – Where did I come from?, Why am I here?, Where am I going?, and Who am I? – and appreciate each answer at any time, any place, by anyone.

"Immortality is the single word I chose to reflect these thoughts."

In due time, the pieces of paper with the words we had written were gathered together. Then, each person choose from the group which was held with the blank side facing toward them. We didn't know what word we had chosen until we turned the paper over.

Many of us immediately saw a connection between the word we had written and the word we received. The word on my sheet was con-nectedness. Connectedness is a word I often hear Dr. Daniel use in his teaching so it is a concept that I have given considerable thought to. Even so, when I read the word on this piece of paper, my mind opened to the realization that immortality in the now, the present, *is* the realization of connectedness between and within Self and all of creation.

As we discussed what we had given and received, many had illumi-nating experiences filled with bold insights and new ways of looking at ourselves and our world.

Here are the words we chose.

community	*spiritual*	*transcendence*
betterment	*kindness*	*eternity*
reverence	*service*	*goodness*
balance	*evolvement*	*stillness*
truth	*purposefulness*	*conscience*
being	*immortality*	*compassion*
awareness	*learning*	

Two people said love, and four said connectedness.

These values we saw this day told us a story about ourselves as individuals and as a group. Some remarked that they could see many of these thoughts in the long-form descriptions they had written. Perhaps you can too.

The people gathered today in the Peace Dome had come from eight states, all for the purpose of learning and teaching metaphysics. The depth of their thinking, the diversity and commonality of their ideas, reflect this. When you study what each gave and received, you can readily see the Universal Laws of creation and attraction working in these people's lives. It is an amazing delight!

Here are the thoughts about ancient values that sustain us.

Carrie Collins
The golden rule. Do unto others as you would have them do unto you.
Love can be experienced by all.
Take care of your family.
There is always a better way to go about things.
Be a good person and you will have wealth in the after life.
I have never even thought about this at all, but now that I'm thinking
about this there is one main thing. I think that most people have a
sense of karma and dharma—what they're here to give—That they
have an idea that they have something to learn and something to give.
It's the inner urge.

The word I received...Betterment.
The word I gave...Balance.

Paul Madar

Throughout the course of human evolution, what has sustained mankind has been a continual quest for <u>betterment</u>. This has taken many forms, many qualities, has sparked many unions, marriages, alliances, the misinterpretation of this urge has led to wars, separation and the concepts of "my country", "my city", "my stuff".

At its essence, betterment is the hope, the faith that effort will produce an evolution of some sort, whether internal or external. It takes the form of value of <u>education</u>, <u>spiritual evolution</u>, <u>freedom</u> to live, choose, and become, and <u>cooperation</u> with others. All of these lead, hopefully, to the betterment of Self, community and thereby human condition.

The word I gave... betterment
The word I received... connectedness

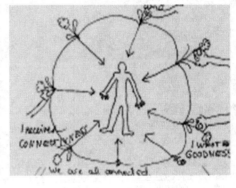

Sharka Glet
Ancient Values are:
They are laws created to promote the goodness. They always focus on the betterment of the whole . They include people and their freedom to experience and grow spiritually.

I received connectedness
I wrote goodness

Mari Hamersley...
When I am honest
I respect my Self   I give my Self I love my Self   I imagine more   I live Truth forming faith Acting with devotion   Disciplined Commitment Learning to live Fully and deeply   Integrity binds   The All to gether Mind, heart. Body, soul, spirit   Connected as One Bringing God's peace   In joy and gratitude Fulfillment.

Honesty, respect, love, truth, commitment, Integrity, Discipline, Wisdom, Peace, Connectedness, Joy Compassion, Giving, Sharing One's self, Faith, Devotion, Imagining, Learning & growth

Inviting into me the mind of God. The urge for <u>goodness</u> is really reaching for <u>connectedness</u>
These show the kind of thinkers we are. Caring. Golden rule: What you do to others you do to yourself. Its <u>Connectedness.</u> As I love, I do to myself   Personal Benefit & connectedness

Dr. Sheila Benjamin...
Love is at the core of our Being
Growing as we share it with others
Bringing us closer to our Divine Source
Finding that Breath is Eternal
and light is Everlasting
Love   Light   Connection Giving and Receiving   Loyalty
Awareness of a Source Greater to reach for

Community

Matthew D. Marian...

1. Self Respect
2. Undivided Attention
3. Concentration
4. Memory
5. Listening
6. Imagination
7. Breath
8. Reasoning
9. Intuition
10. Entrainment

The Essential Life Skills
are a scientific means by
which humankind reaches
mastery. They have been
taught in one form or
another for eons of time.
These skills are the
wellspring of all virtue.
These skills build in their
practitioner all that
humankind deems
valuable.

The word I gave...Learning
The word I received...
Transcendence

Marsha Craig...
Goodness and happiness, ancient values that have sustained mankind
unconditional Love—pure acceptance for past, present and future.
Desire to grow, learn and achieve—move forward Positive outlook/
optimism. Positive role models and teachers. Giving service.

The word I gave... Love
The word I received... Learning

Valerie Blomgren...
Ancient Values
Finding indiscriminating love within everyone.
Understanding one's purpose for existing, by
giving, loving, helps elevate consciousness.
Understanding fluid connection among each
individual.
Encourage growth in humanity.

Purposefulness
Truth

John Mestyanek...
The Ancient Values that have Sustained mankind:
Brotherhood/Community   Openness
Love   Respect   Curiosity
Caring   Altruism   Understanding
Compassion   Working together   Friendship
Support

Gave— Community
Received—Reverence

Greg Brown...
<u>*The ones who figure it out...so few*</u>

Know thyself as a spirit
To know we are Creators in flesh and our goal is mastery of self, of consciousness to know our own spirit. Ultimately this is what the ancient ones left behind in all scriptures and this is what sustains mankind. The ability to think deeply, contemplate, question and understand why we are here and where we are going when the chains of reincarnation are relieved.

Transcendence
kindness

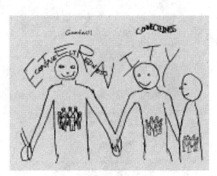

Adam Campbell...
The Circle of Love   Namaste
Seeing eye to eye   Heart to Heart
Goodwill

Connectedness
Eternity

Karen Mosby...
Seek to be of service to everyone you meet.
Treat others as you wish to be treated
Love one another
Seek to understand each other
Give to those in need There is a higher source than us that guides us and sustains us.
We all are here for a purpose—we all have value.
We are connected to each other and to everything
We all desire the same things in life
Peace, enough, Value, love
Follow your heart —your inner wisdom

Shawn Stoner...
Belief in a Higher Being/ Intelligence/ Force or Power
We are all connected— What I do to you, I do to myself
There is a center of goodness within all beings
Understanding
Love is Universal

The word I gave...Spiritual
The word I received... Awareness

Word written <u>Connectedness</u>
Received Love

Dory Wheatley...
Kindness   openness   love   honesty
generosity   vision   simplicity   Love (what I received)

As a Christmas gift I made my sister a calendar with photos and artwork of my children—Iris & Ella. There were also quotes from people with wisdom. My sister is weary of, repelled, almost afraid of religion —even spirituality.

On one of the pages there is a picture of infant Ella gazing openly into her Aunt Cathleen's face. Cathleen is holding her very tenderly, very lovingly. The photo was black and white, cut into the shape of a heart and circled in a simple pink line. Beside it was a quote from the Dalai Lama. It ended with "...my only religion, kindness." My sister cried when she read this. I knew it touched her soul. The Dalai Lama can do that, with what he embodies. He includes everyone.

The list of ancient values I made can all be seen within them. They sustain mankind. The word – "kindness."

Erika Scholz...
We are all connected.
We are all one.
Love is our nature.
Love all.
Give freely.
Treat others the way you wish to be treated.

Connectedness
Compassion

Tad Messenger...
Goodness and happiness for all mankind
The sustained ancient values are for <u>reverence</u>, <u>balance</u>.
A reverence for creation for nature and for people's of the earth.
The thought of <u>love</u> for all mankind. Love ye one another.
We are all in this together—<u>Connectedness</u> — what you give, you receive.
<u>Karma</u> & <u>Dharma</u>
What you learn what you give to the whole

<u>gratitude</u> & <u>forgiveness</u>

I chose reverence
I received balance

Dr. Daniel R. Condron....
The ancient values that have sustained mankind.

1. Caring about the well-being of others.
2. Nurturing love at an early age
3. The family of Father, Mother and children
4. Believe in a higher consciousness or Heaven
5. Truth and honesty

Do unto others as you would have them do unto you.

The word I chose = connectedness
The word I received was — Evolvement

Terryll Nemeth...
I am told that I can help
An echo from my inner urge resounds
The voice is loud and true.
I discover what I am here to do.

Love dwells within
Compassion expresses the heart
Truth reveals itself with expanded
attention
Still mind is birthed from creation.

One word – Being
Goodness

Dave Rosemann...
Connectedness
<u>The ancient values that have sustained Mankind</u>
Peace is our true nature.
Everyone desires to be happy.
We are all part of one connected community called humanity.
Love is at the essence of all things.
We all desire to learn and progress, aiding one another to evolve
Each person's thoughts and actions effect the whole

Eternity

V
A
L
U
E

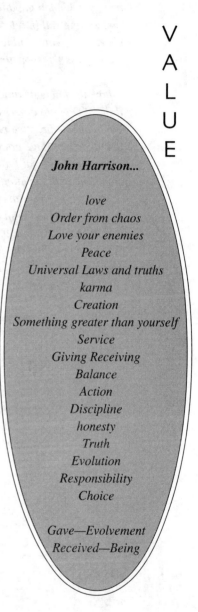

John Harrison...

love
Order from chaos
Love your enemies
Peace
Universal Laws and truths
karma
Creation
Something greater than yourself
Service
Giving Receiving
Balance
Action
Discipline
honesty
Truth
Evolution
Responsibility
Choice

Gave—Evolvement
Received—Being

Dr. Laurel Clark...
Love   Truth
beauty   human goodness   happiness   caring for others
recognizing self in relationship to the whole   consideration   Respect   kindness
charity   loving kindness   generosity   service   gratitude   forgiveness   dedication
willingness   responsibility   goodness

I think the ancient values that have sustained mankind can be summed up in the Golden Rule: "Do unto others as you would have them do unto you."
When people practice respect - putting themselves in another's shoes, seeing things from the other's vantage point, feeling what someone else feels. They can have compassion.
All of the Universal Laws are these ancient values so when people can still their minds to commune with the mind of the Creation, they can respond to a natural sense of conscience. I believe that conscience is drawing upon the inner urge to be like our Creator. It is the alignment with Superconciousness and the conscious response to that. When we aid other people to abundance, we have abundance ourselves. When we give, we receive. When we seek first the Kingdom of Heaven – our own divinity – all else is given to us. Knowing that we're all in this together makes it simpler to realize our importance in what we think, what we say, what we do, how we live. Our duty is to be our best in how we influence others.
I wrote and received Conscience.

Terry Martin...
Love of Self and others   Respect for all life
Compassion and connectedness   Reverence and devotion
Love includes teaching and expectation. Virtue and grace,
faith and charity. Love is all. The alpha and omega.
Love—I wrote
Purposefulness—I received

Laurie J. Biswell...
Ancient Values are the foundation of who we are, where we came from, why we are here and where we are going. It is the Universal Laws and Truths activated. It is giving more than what we expect from others. Faith, devotion, tranquility, Peace, when all is said and done what we have is each other. The connectedness that we are all created in the image and likeness of the Creator.

I gave Connectedness
I received Stillness

John Crainshaw...

To me ancient values are simple truths that every person alive can tune into. "All he need do is quiet the mind and know." Open up any Holy Work ever written and you will find them. Visit an old religious temple or building and you can absorb them into your being. Speak with any Master Teacher and see that their whole life revolves around these truths. I'm not going to tell you that I know these truths to be. All the words have already been written, spoken or prayed. I encourage any seeker of truth to look within Self to reveal the ultimate authority and truth in the universe.

Gave —Stillness
Received—Spiritual

Jay McCormick...

Ancient Values that sustain mankind for millennia
The whole is greater than the sum of its parts
Everyone working together
produces a synthesis that
Ignites creativity and energy to
produce and innovate mentally,
emotionally and physically to
solve challenges and grow

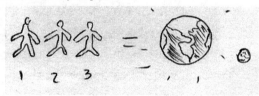

The willingness to be of service to the whole to place
the needs of the many above the needs of the one.

Service
Service

Dr. Pam Blosser...

There is a benevolence at the core of Creation
Sentient beings have a reason for being here something to overcome
Love, compassion, right thoughts, actions are the way
to learn/understand/overcome
We are all connected to something much greater
than any of us individually
Thinking of the well-being of others expands all of us.
Also acting on these ideas
Give to those less fortunate
Live to the best you can imagine.
Your mistakes must be corrected to align with that which is greater.

I wrote – compassion
I receive – connectedness

The Peace Dome under construction late Spring 2003.

There are two floors to the Peace Dome. The second floor is a complete chamber unto itself where the expanse of the shape can be fully experienced. Your eyes are filled with a white sky that radiates above you with portals into space at the zenith. Your ears resonate with the whispers that come back to you so you may listen to your own thoughts. The energy here moves continuously, giving back to you what you give. It is an amazing space where ancient values come alive.

You reach the second floor by climbing a ramp that is supported by the Healing Wall. The Healing Wall includes a 9x20 foot relief map of the continents of our planet created by the children of Camp Niangua in 2003. The map will in time become the home of stones from every country in the world, the first place of its kind to bring Mother Earth together in such a way.

Over two dozen windows open the first floor to the world. The opening in the dome is an ellipse. Although the opening was present from the inflation of the dome, the airform had remained intact stretching like a window shade attached on all sides. Cutting open this airform was a symbolic act of giving this structure to the world. We were literally, physically, opening the Dome to the world.

Those of us who live here, who are building the Peace Dome, caring for it daily, live with the sense that the Peace Dome belongs to the world. It is not just a building on the campus of the College of Metaphysics. It both represents and is something greater than each of us.

When we cut the Dome open on a snowy Sunday in March, it was an amazing moment of equanimity – the sweet and the bitter, coming and going, the past and the future. As we took turns making the opening larger, all of us felt it in the transition in a most profound way.

As the Dome moves through its stages it takes on the quality of a sacred site, one people will dream about visiting from the time of their childhood and will journey many miles to experience.   Indeed, this is already happening as the Dome is being constructed. People come from California and Maryland and Wisconsin, sometimes not really knowing why until they see the Peace Dome and hear its story.

I can imagine pilgrimages from every part of the globe to the hamlet of Windyville, Missouri, for the express purpose of being, praying, breathing in the Peace Dome. Perhaps this is why when I read the words of the Dalai Lama, I resonate with them.

"It is my dream that the entire Tibetan plateau should become a free refuge where humanity and nature can live in peace and in harmonious balance. It would be a place where people from all over the world could come to seek the true meaning of peace within themselves, away from the tensions and pressures of much of the rest of the world. Tibet could indeed become a creative center for the promotion and development of peace."

As will, I whole-heartedly believe, the Peace Dome.

Before
&
After

Footnotes from *Lesson Six*

27-30 From His Holiness the Dalai Lama of Tibet's acceptance speech given upon receipt of the Nobel Peace Prize, December 11, 1989 in Oslo, Norway.

To learn more about the history of the Peace Dome visit
www.peacedome.org

What is friendship?
Lisa Bold

Friendship is very unconditional. I accept my friends
unconditionally and they accept me unconditionally
where we're at in our learning. It's someone to communicate with
so I understand my thoughts more and understand Universal Truth. Friendship is
having friends to experience with, someone I know that
I can rely in.

Friendship is giving and receiving unconditionally

Receiving
At first my mind was busy — I was a little uncomfortable — and
after a few people I stilled my mind and received what each individual was giving
me. I was filled with so much joy and love.

Giving — I have an easier time with. I felt very connected
and received by the individuals I was giving to. I was filled
with love and gratitude for the experience.

What is friendship?
Pam Blosser

knowing you can let all the walls down   honesty
understanding   allowing   enriches because you allow the doors
and windows of your mind to be open
is the bestower of good things between people
and brings out the best between / among people
is fanning the eternal flame of benevolence and love and all good things
* Friendship fans the eternal flame of all good things.
Namaste — saluting the divinity in another

Giving — opened my heart to them as I gave and experienced when
they received it

Receiving — could receive their words — their learning that
reflected in their words — and themselves — could receive
them — experienced the resonance of truth
coming from each one

What is friendship?
Marlena Garrison 8/3/2003

Devotion to a common ideal with love and Truth
given and received freely.

* Devotion for love and Truth.

Receiving — I received each person, their essence, heart and soul.
Mentally, emotionally what their ideal of friendship is.

Giving — I received back what I gave — that connection ,
the ideal of friendship is in my mind. And I received the person
as they received. I gave my ideal of friendship — my image
apart of myself — where I don't always give
of my whole Self.
It — I felt complete.

Aaron

Friendship can be as broad as a person desires.
Some like to have only a few close friends
while others are loners. "I am my own best friend," say they.
Then there are those who consider all the world their friends.

Friendship is a commitment to grow and enjoy life together.

We are one. The deeper this truth is expressed
in friendships the greater the fulfillment.
If we can see that we are not really one
with our closest friends, but all are one
then we can live life with far fuller friends.

Friendship is growing into awareness
with another individual.

PEACEMAKINGPEACEMAKINGPEACEMAKINGPEACEMAKING

Lesson Seven

IDEAL

"Peace
is the breath of our spirit..."

"All men are created equal and are endowed by their Creator with certain inalienable rights," wrote Thomas Jefferson in his drafts of the Declaration of Independence for the founding of a new nation. Being born in the United States, these inherent freedoms have given me the space to grow and change as an individual. On this PeaceMakers I would come to appreciate this in a new light.

In 1979, I believed the Nobel laureate we studied today to be an indecisive leader who had let our country down. I was in my mid-20's and I did not understand how a small country like Iran could hold a nation like the United States hostage for weeks. I was idealistic and not yet pragmatic. Time and experience has broadened my capacity to understand and this morning as I read the complete text of Jimmy Carter's acceptance speech for the 2002 Nobel Peace Prize, I found myself humbled for I realized how much I had changed.

When introducing Carter, the Chairman of the Norwegian Nobel Committee, Gunnar Berge, said the peace prize was being awarded to Jimmy Carter for *"his decades of untiring effort to find peaceful solutions to international conflicts, to advance democracy and human rights, and to promote economic and social development."*

Berge went on to describe Carter as the politician who attempted to bring about a more peaceful world. In 1978, during his one term as president of the United States, he mediated peace accords between the leaders of Israel and Egypt. These two men shared the peace prize that year. After leaving political office, Berge noted that Carter continues to seek peaceful solutions to international conflicts often engaging in disarmament and arms control talks. His humanitarian and social activities have demonstrated an outstanding commitment to democracy and human rights throughout his life.

In references to gross national products and superpowers, Carter's acceptance speech reflected the broad governmental circles he has traveled for seven decades – always as peacemaker.

Referring to the dissolution of the Soviet Union, he notes that now there is only one superpower. But instead of this assuring stability and freedom, *"instead of entering a millennium of peace, the world is now, in many ways, a more dangerous place."* He speaks of the large numbers of civil wars in Europe, Asia, and Africa, bringing to our attention that many of the casualties are unarmed civilians with no ability to defend themselves. He talks of terrorism saying that global challenges must be met with an emphasis on peace, in harmony with others, with strong alliances and international consensus. This from a man whose first chosen occupation was in the military as a submarine officer.

Like so many of the laureates, Carter has a command of the juxtapositioning of man's potential and his reality. He describes the challenges we face by superimposing the physical condition with the mental condition. For instance he says the *"the greater ease of travel and communication has not been matched by equal understanding and mutual respect"* between nations. In this way, he identifies the cause of what ails mankind while highlighting the cure for the dis-ease that afflicts us.

Carter speaks of his time as president of a superpower as *"a constant and delicate balancing of our great military strength with aggressive diplomacy, always seeking to build friendships with other nations, large and small, that shared a common cause."*[31] It is this simple clarity of idealism that forms my more expanded – and I believe more compassionate and truthful – view of Jimmy Carter. His command of world situations is direct, honest, and simple because he can face what is while holding onto an idea of what can be.

When describing the world as he sees it, there is a strong sense of the man that he is. This is more pervasive than his ideas. In fact it is very clear that his ideas stem from his character. He could have changed his mind back in 1979, bent to public opinion, and been reelected for it. Instead he, like Gandhi before him, remained true to his ideals, his life becoming the testament to the truth he lives.

When we look at the lives of both of these world leaders we find the seeds of their destiny in their early years. The source for the people they became is found in their early formative years. Gandhi's mother gave him instruction in Jainism, an amazing religion of ahimsa (nonviolence), forgiveness, self-discipline, and service. Carter's mother gave Jimmy a strong Christian ethic encompassing the same values. Perhaps it is the strength of faith in Carter's early years, as it was with Gandhi, that enables him to see what eludes others and to be steadfast in holding to his ideals.

In his acceptance speech Carter mentions lessons learned from Julia Coleman, a childhood teacher. She introduced him to the novel, *War and Peace* by Leo Tolstoy – whose book *The Kingdom of God is Within You* greatly influenced Gandhi. Her interpretation of Tolstoy's work that the simple human attributes of goodness and truth can overcome great power made an impression on Carter.

"She also taught us that an individual is not swept along on a tide of inevitability but can influence even the greatest human events."[32] It is this truth that forms a new concept of individual idealism that Carter cites by listing previous Nobel laureates. From Norman Borlaug to Aung San Suu Kyi to Mother Teresa, these peace prize winners might have been little known outside their own regions without Nobel recognition. His words reflect what he learned to be true as a child. *"All of these and others have proven that even without government power - and often in opposition to it - individuals can enhance human rights and wage peace, actively and effectively."*[33]

This thought was so amazing to me. So simple in its intent. Carter seemed to be introducing a new kind of hero, one beyond the old archetypal images. This hero is inclusive in his thinking and creative in his manner. He or she possesses the ability to perceive the common cause of all people.

This sense of common good among many undoubtedly stems from his strong sense of family. One of the most enduring choices the 2002 Nobel Peace Prize laureate made was marrying Rosalynn. In 1975, in his book *Why Not the Best?* he described them as "full partners" writing, "When we decided to enter politics, Rosalynn helped me from every standpoint." Like Gandhi before him, Carter derives strength, insight, and support from his wife.

Perhaps his strong sense of family, both personal and universal, shines most brightly when he elucidates the following truth:

"War may sometimes be a necessary evil. But no matter how necessary, it is always an evil, never a good. We will not learn how to live together in peace by killing each other's children."[34]

Certainly many a mother has come to this same conclusion time and time again. Yet killing persists often with, as Betty Williams asserted, women as the instigators. Many religions teach that life is sacred and taking life deplored. Yet many murders are committed in the name of religious Gods.

What will stop us from killing each other?

Since the question has been asked over and over for generations without benefit of real progress, perhaps it is time to amend the question.

There is a wonderful Sufi story that illustrates very well the realization of this universal need.

One evening Mulla – which means teacher in Persian – was outside his hut, bent over with hands filing through the dust of the ground. His persistence gained the attention of a woman returning from market. She stopped and asked, "What are you doing?"

"I have lost the key to a great treasure," Mulla replied.

"A great treasure!" exclaimed the poor woman, thinking that if she found the key perhaps the teacher would be grateful and share the treasure. "Let me help you."

Soon a man came by and seeing the two crawling in the dust he asked, "What are you doing?"

The woman replied, "We are searching for the key that has been lost."

"What is the key to?" the man asked.

"A great treasure," replied the woman.

"I will help you look," said the man and he quickly fell on his hands and knees.

Next a group of villagers on their way home for the night came upon the trio. "Why are you crawling on the ground?"

"We are searching for a key to a great treasure," said the helpers.

"A great treasure?" replied one of the villagers. "Let us all assist you in this important task! Perhaps when we find it, we can all share it!"

A large crowd was now crawling in the dust and grass, looking for the key. Night was quickly falling. Since this was making it more difficult to see, a young boy moved closer to Mulla and asked, "Are you certain that you dropped the key right here?"

Mulla stopped for a moment and replied, "No. I lost the key some-where in my house."

Upon hearing this the crowd of villagers exclaimed, "Have you gone mad? If the key is in your house, why are you searching for it out here?"

"Because it was light out here," Mulla replied. "Inside the house there is no light."

Someone then asked, "Even if the light is here, how can we find the key if it has not been lost here?"

One of the people, holding great pride in their theories, said, "It seems that if you bring light inside the house you can find the key, teacher."

Mulla laughed.

"Indeed it is the simple question and simple answer which brings illumination," he said. "You are such clever people about small things. You are helpful and industrious, yet your efforts seem to fail to produce what you want. Yet, when one of you formed the question that would bring you the insight you needed your efforts were seen in a new light! One simple truth, one additional question, told you what you wanted to know.

"So it is your inner life. I have seen all of you searching outside. By helping me you have learned from your experience. As you have learned here, today, what you are seeking is not lost without, it has always been within. Why seek bliss in the outside world? Have you lost it there?" [35]

Asking questions opens the mind to possibilities. To prepare for today's task of describing an ideal of peace, we began by turning our attention inward. We did this by listing one hundred questions. Sound easy?

Try it right now.

Take a pen and several sheets of paper. Now think of questions you have about life. Begin by writing the first ideas that come to your mind. Don't stop to analyze or judge your thoughts, once you begin just keep going until you reach 100.

Start now.

By listing questions that come to mind we begin a process of cleansing. The first 25 questions empty the mind of everyday clutter: "Why am I trying to think of questions? Why a hundred? What am I supposed to put down? What are they looking for? How long will this take? What if I can't come up with 100 questions?"

These questions begin to give way to more insightful ones. The next 25 allow us to go deeper, exploring more meaningful, often nonphysical concepts and emotional impressions. "Why is this making me nervous? Why is it so hard for me to say what I want? Why can't I forgive and forget? Why can't I remember certain things? Did my mother know how much I loved her?"

In the third set of 25 universal themes surface – life, death, love, justice, hope. "What is my purpose in life? What is the purpose in life? What is goodness? Why is there evil in the world? Is there a God?" Our minds have opened beyond the limits of our own experience.

The final 25 questions reveal repeated themes that bring new insight as they surface from a deeper place in Self. Often these revolve around four major questions of existence: "Where did I come from? Why am I here? Where am I going? and Who am I?"

Some found once they began the questions poured from their minds, one after another. Others found they got stuck, usually around those 25 increment times. Some wrote 100 questions in fifteen minutes, others took an hour. There is no right or wrong to this exercise, merely the ability to fulfill it, then reflect upon what the accomplishing revealed.

A common experience among those who do this exercise is a relaxing of the outer mind, so the inner mind can come forward with greater clarity. By the time we completed our questions, we were ready to explore our ideals.

Centuries later a modern day teacher came to the same conclusion as Mulla, saying, *"Our problem today is that we have allowed the internal to become lost in the external."*

Martin Luther King, Jr., a fellow Georgian Carter holds in high esteem, believed that each person is dual, living in two realms, the internal

and the external. He saw the internal as a realm expressed in art, literature, morals and religion. Here are the realm of ideas like "do unto others
as you would have them do unto you" or "thou shalt not kill" which seeks
to connect all of us in favorable regard for each other. This realm exists for
spiritual ends.

The external realm King described as a "complex of devices, techniques, mechanisms and instruments" which are the means by which we
live. Imagine! This he spoke years before technology became a dominant
factor in our lives. Even in 1964, telephones, televisions, motorized ve-
hicles, appliances and the like were changing the way we see ourselves and
the way we live. Given this, the timelessness of his words testifies to the
universal truth contained within them.

*"Our problem today is that we have allowed the internal to become lost in
the external. We have allowed the means by which we live to outdistance
the ends for which we live. So much of modern life can be summarized in
that arresting dictum of the poet Thoreau: 'Improved means to an unim-
proved end'."*[36]

King saw this as the serious predicament of modern man. Think of it this
way, what is in the mind of the religious man who has been taught and
believes that killing is wrong when his government, his family, even his
minister tells him he must fight for or defend his country? King called such
situations of contradiction deep and haunting saying that if we are to survive, *"our moral and spiritual 'lag' must be eliminated."*

Learning how to ask the right questions for the answers we are
seeking bridges this gap between the spiritual and material worlds. Instead of asking "what will stop us from killing each other" perhaps we need
to explore why most of us never resort to murder. We need to ask, "Why is
it so easy for me to forgive my best friend?" "How come my friend can
criticize-tease-get-angry-at-me one minute and the next we are laughing
and having a great time?" "Why is it so easy for my best friend to accept
people as they are? be considerate of other's feelings? let things go?"
These questions open the mind and heart to a deeper understanding. They
mend the moral/spiritual lag.

Learning how to ask questions is the beginning of learning how to communicate. Listening is its companion. As a way to prepare ourselves for this morning's exercise, we paired off and spent some time asking questions and listening to each other. We began with the question, "What is most important to you?"

What we learned about ourselves and each other reflected the influence of our daily practice of concentration and meditation. The answers ranged from God to love, from family to independence. Some said, "knowing myself" while others talked about being at peace. Most of the answers were Self reflective, and most focused in some way on making the world a better place.

Concentration enables you to still your mind, focusing on giving or receiving. The still mind is free of prejudice, anger, blame, depression, resentment, and the host of negativities that disturb our capacity for peace. The still mind can open to another person or to the inner Self, receiving what is offered.

Meditation connects the outer Self with the inner Self, what many describe today as the head and the heart. The power of the outer Self is reasoning. The power of the inner Self is intuition. By harmonizing these two parts of mind, a super consciousness is produced. When both are employed as a daily discipline, thinking stretches, deepens, develops, and matures. People, places, and things are perceived from many perspectives thus broadening your point of view. In this frame of mind – what Albert Schweitzer called a "new mentality" – you are ready to contemplate a spiritual concept like peace. This is how an ideal is created.

Albert Schweitzer eloquently described mankind's long-term fascination with peace. He noted that peoples who have reached a certain level of civilization dream of a lasting peace.

"In Palestine it appeared for the first time in the words of the prophet Amos in the eighth century B.C., and it continues to live in the Jewish and Christian religions as the belief in the Kingdom of God. It figures in the doctrine taught by the great Chinese thinkers: Confucius and Lao-tse in the sixth century B.C., Mi-tse in the fifth, and Meng-tse in the fourth. It reappears in Tolstoy and in other contemporary European thinkers. People have labeled it a utopia. But the situation today is such that it must become reality in one way or another; otherwise mankind will perish."[37]

Schweitzer said these words in 1952.

Schweitzer was not a pessimist. His life was filled with positive action from living with natives in French Equatorial Africa to performing music in Western cities in order to elevate awareness and raise funds. He reiterated many times his belief that the human spirit is capable of creating in what he called a new mentality. He noted that many truths have lain unnoticed for a long time, ignored simply because no one perceives their potential for becoming reality.

The beauty of the Nobel Peace laureates is the reality of their idealism. They do not portend to know all the answers. Rather they do their work in the world with devotion and steadfastness. Some call them pragmatic idealists. Certainly they are individuals with high ideals who are committed to living them.

I remember a quote I read when I was 15 that was attributed to Sen. Robert F. Kennedy, "Some people see things as they are and say, 'Why?' I dream of things that never were and say, 'Why not?'" It was kind of a backdoor way into realizing a vision of what can be, but I got the message and I remember over three decades later. By asking questions, Kennedy was defining universal ideals.

Idealistic people share a broad vision of the place spirit holds in the progress of human beings. I have noticed in my studies and travels that the greatest thinkers among us are often well-read, being particularly well-versed in scriptures of the world. King was an example of this as was Alva Myrdal. When Gandhi died, the three books he counted in his few possessions were the *Bhagavad Gita*, the *Koran*, and the *Bible*.

This vision of truth that is universal expresses itself in Carter's thinking. Just as those who strive for peace can be said to be color-blind concerning race, so they may be described as dogma-deaf concerning religion and culture. Carter recognized that all religions share "*common commitments that define our ideal secular relationships. I am convinced that Christians, Muslims, Buddhists, Hindus, Jews, and others can embrace each other in a common effort to alleviate human suffering and to espouse peace.*"[38]

"Ideal secular relationships."

In order to strive for peace, we must create a vision of peace that affects our daily interactions. It must be more than the denial of what we do not want, what we do not like in ourselves or others. His Holiness the Dalai Lama says,

"Peace, in the sense of the absence of war, is of little value to someone who is dying of hunger or cold. It will not remove the pain of torture inflicted on a prisoner of conscience. It does not comfort those who have lost their loved ones in floods caused by senseless deforestation in a neighbouring country. Peace can only last where human rights are respected, where the people are fed, and where individuals and nations are free."39

Our ideal of peace must exceed what has existed previously. A vision beyond the norm, beyond the average, is called for to bring about a new world. It must bring new ways of thinking into our consciousness, for as it states so concisely in the *Universal Peace Covenant* – "living peaceably begins by thinking peacefully." In 530 words it describes what peace is, what causes peace in the individual and in the world.

The *Universal Peace Covenant* is this common vision for all sentient beings.

I have read many historical documents throughout my life, and certainly this one is worthy of every human being. With only two references to what peace is not, reading the *Covenant* is like eating the purest, finest, richest meal. It leaves you wanting more even when you are full. Assimilating it deserves intelligence and time.

At the beginning of 2003, many of us made a commitment to ourselves and each other to read the *Covenant* daily. The impact the *Universal Peace Covenant* has had on our lives was apparent at PeaceMakers this day, when we endeavored to articulate our ideals by completing the thought "Peace is......". Thought exercises such as these strengthen what Schweitzer called the new mentality. With each opportunity to respond we think more deeply which gives energy to the new vision.

What is peace to you? Here are some of our thoughts.

*...movement in and around and through
goodness for all concerned. Peace is truth.
Peace is being dedicated to something greater then ourselves, and
knowing our efforts are making a difference in the world, humanity or those
close to ourselves. Peace begins with giving
because that connects us to our essence,
and to each other. –Pam Blosser*

*..... helping others. All Nobel prize winners helped people, many
people. Peace is receptive. –Daniel Condron*

*....the pulse of the universe. Peace is a face of love. Peace
disintegrates fear, anger, doubts and insecurities. It con-
nects us with the essence of creation.
Peace is:
Spiritual communion. Giving light to the world.
My true nature with God. Connectedness.
The breath of the Creator.
–John Mestyanek*

*...the Universal Peace Covenant magnified to infinity.
Peace is the Universal Peace Covenant embodied by all sentient
beings. Peace is simple, truth and love. –Christine Madar*

*....understanding. It comes from a still mind. Inner peace is when
the mind is aligned with universal law. Peace among people
occurs when each individual is aligned with superconsciousness,
when people give themselves to a common ideal that is greater
than themselves, serving humanity, serving God, serving a greater
whole produces peace. Understanding cause within the self
produces inner and outer peace. Intentionally causing light
(awareness) to increase produces peace. –Laurel Clark*

....mental connectedness, emotional accord, physical unity and spiritual communion. Peace is developed within, reflected and lived outward toward our neighbor and the world. –Teresa Padilla

.....awareness of connectedness and personal responsibility. At some time the laureates had an experience of expanded awareness and they realized their connectedness. From this stimulus they chose to use their lives to serve humanity by manifesting their personal visions for peace. Each of us have the power to nurture a personal vision for peace. As more of us make this choice, peace will move across the face of the Earth. I AM HE. –Matthew Marian

Peace is best expressed by the Universal Peace Covenant. This document relates the truth of peace in ways that are vibrant and resonate with the soul. To me, peace is coming home. It is my true nature when I am still and with God. Peace can be received through the 5 senses. However, peace can only be known through the Self. I have an image of spiritual intuitive man, and a vital part of that image is peace throughout all levels of mind. As peace moves through each of us, may it be magnified and reflected to the 144,000. May peace prevail on Earth. –Erika Scholz

"Peace is the breath of our spirit, it wells up from within the depths of our being to refresh, to heal, to inspire." Peace is the internal energy that connects everyone and everything. It is the universal pulse connecting us to one another. Peace is the resonance that blend tones together creating harmony with one another. Peace is alignment with the ideal that the Creator is always with us. It is knowing that peace is creation. "Peace is active. The motion of, silence of, faith, of accord, of service. It is not written in documents, but in the hearts and minds of men and women." Peace is universal, and within every being on the planet. –Laurie Biswell

Peace is...

...at its essence what we call understanding. When I am upset I am not at peace. I find myself reacting to the world and everyone around me. In a while, after I have distracted myself with sensory thrills, or time has passed, I don't feel the emotion anymore, but it is still there. It will rear its head again soon. I am still not at peace with myself and my neighbor. When I seek the truth and understand why, I learn the lesson in it for me. Then, it has been my experience, through the divine order of the universe, the conditions which upset me before I barely take notice. –John Crainshaw

....knowing your real self, and being secure in who you are. To realize this you allow yourself to be connected and in harmony with others, for in knowing others we will know ourselves. Peace is loving others as well as yourself. –John Harrison

There is a breath from the Creator that pervades all life. It envelops within and between every molecule, every thought, every interaction. It is this breath that brings motion, stability and security to our existence. It is the Creator's breath that is the peace of our spirit. When I was a child and a teenager, during every trying time I used to say, "It will work out, it will be okay." This thought came from my connection with the breath of our spirit, the Creator's breath. This is the peace that I find within me. –Tad Messenger

.... actually bringing forth what will bring greater light to the world. Just as the sun is most brilliant as it shines among clouds, individual's needs shine brightest when serving the needs of others. –Terry Martin

....the breath of God.

The Universal Peace Covenant describes the elemental principles of peace, a blueprint for what Pauling describes as a "culture worthy of man's intelligence", the guiding thoughts that manifest. What the Dalai Lama calls the "universal responsibility for one another and the planet we share." Peace is the fruit of conscious soul living.
–Barbara Condron

Exploring peace is a worthy pastime. To understand its attractiveness is to experience freedom – for what you may not have today you can very well have tomorrow. The open mind entertains possibilities, the "what ifs"? What if there is another choice? What if we allow both red and green, young and old, rich and poor? What if we are, as His Holiness the Dalai Lama says so eloquently, *"all basically the same human beings?"*

The Dalai Lama acknowledges the same basic needs and concerns shared by all humans. We seek happiness. We go to extreme lengths to avoid suffering. We prize freedom highly, wanting the right to determine our own destiny. People are hungry for self-determination, and self-determination fosters thinking. People may experience this newfound inner urge as fighting against what is until they realize the power they fear they have lost or do not have has been within them all along.

We find this power by going within the mind, by using our intelligence and will toward higher ideals. This is exercising freedom. The concept that freedom is the ability to do whatever you want makes sense only in a world where selfish desires have been transcended. Freedom in its higher manifestation is the realization that your thought is creative.

Jimmy Carter describes it in this way, *"The bond of our common humanity is stronger than the divisiveness of our fears and prejudices. God gives us the capacity for choice. We can choose to alleviate suffering. We can choose to work together for peace. We can make these changes - and we must."* 40

Asking questions is the beginning of freedom, of communication, of acceptance, of expansion in our own minds. It is the reason humanity prizes education so highly. The highest form of education manifests the spirit of the word. *Educatus,* from which educate is derived, means to bring up, to draw out. The mind that can form questions wants to know. Its owner has already made room – past the limits of past experience – for the new.

"Why did I say that?"

"Do others understand what I am trying to say?"

"Am I expressing my thoughts clearly so they can be understood?"

"Are my thoughts and words in alignment, the same, or am I holding back, editing, or changing the truth I see?"

"What is the truth as I see it?"

"How might I better express that truth?" "Live it?"

Asking such questions is the beginning of the new mentality. This is the mentality of a self-reflective thinker, who desires to see, to learn, to become. Such a one values change because he or she is becoming the change they desire to see. They are idealists.

31-34 Jimmy Carter's Nobel Peace Prize speech © The Nobel Foundation, 2002

35 story adapted from one in <u>Classic Tales of Mulla Nasreddin</u> by Houman Farzad, translated by Diane L. Wilcox (Costa Mesa, CA: Mazda Publishers, 1989)

36 Martin Luther King, Jr. © The Nobel Foundation, 1964

37 Albert Schweitzer © The Nobel Foundation, 1954

38 Jimmy Carter, Ibid.

39 H. H. the Dalai Lama of Tibet © The Nobel Foundation, 1989

40 Jimmy Carter, Ibid.

Jesse Kern

Friendship is universal love experienced
on the personal level between two individuals.

What I received:
It's all true. I felt so full. I felt way powerful receiving with my gaze =
drawing them in. Wow! I loved the intimacy with each one.

What I gave:
Someone asked, "Just two" and I almost changed it
feeling I was wrong but I decided "No this is what I thought
friendship is in that moment" and I gave it,
detaching from the way I perceived it being received.
The intimacy and the intensity of it (the gaze)
was incredible.

What is Friendship
Mari Hamersley

Friendship is a communion between souls.
It is a creation that is built through sharing thought,
emotion, and activity together. It is a oneness of spirit.
Friendship endures because it is a connectedness of souls
which is based on Truth and is, therefore, permanent.
Friendship exists beyond time and space. Friendship is a true
mental concern for what is goodness for all concerned, based on love.

The one sentence definition
**Friendship is the eternal, living connection between souls that produces
wholeness.**

As I received, I felt such deep love for each person and from each person.
And in those I'd just met for the first time (physically) this weekend,
I recognized our soul connection as if I'd known them for eons.
That is universal friendship.

As I gave to each person and said the final word
of my statement "wholeness", I gave myself fully and received
each soul fully. We created wholeness and I was complete
in the love we shared. We expressed in all ways
our eternal, spiritual bond.

What is Friendship?
Laurie Biswell

Sharing, giving, loving, openness

It is a Bond Between Individuals that is always present. THROUGH ALL Things great & small. Friendship is aiding each other to growth & learning. Is the sun place where the earth & the sky meet and sun rises & sets.

Friendship is the Love Shown through A smile.

Receiving — I Felt alive. It is Beautiful to Breathe in each individual's thoughts of What Friendship is. I Felt the love. It was easy For me to Breath in. It was the willingness to give.

Giving — I received so much when I gave, it was an open exchange and almost immediately just about everyone smiled. I could feel the life force energy flow between us and around us. Love was in the air & I knew I was loved.

What is friendship?
Simone Sheehan

Divine Love shared unconditionally given & received between individuals.

In receiving each idea of friendship I received a part of the person giving that will live inside of me. In giving I gave a part of myself that will live with them.
I experienced a true sense of gratitude, because of the abundance of friends I have in my life and because I know I can share this with anyone who crosses my path.

Lesson Eight

PURPOSE

*"True happiness comes
from a sense of inner peace and contentment,
which in turn must be achieved through the
cultivation of altruism, of love and compassion
and elimination of ignorance, selfishness and greed."*

We are all learning on this journey. We are learning that peace is a means to the end as well as the destination. Peace, like love, prosperity, and health, is a condition of mind, a state of mind.

For this PeaceMakers we read about the life of Henri Dunant, the first recipient of the Nobel Peace Prize (1901). A Swiss businessman who had purchased land in the French colony of Algeria, Dunant was on his way to ask permission to pipe water from government-owned property when his life-changing experience awakened his consciousness.

Dunant never made it to see Napoleon III. Instead, he arrived to witness one of the bloodiest battles of the 19th century. The Battle of Solferino on June 24, 1859, claimed 40,000 lives in hand-to-hand slaughter. Dunant joined rescue efforts to evacuate the wounded to a nearby town, working heroically to save lives, direct volunteers, gather food, find doctors, and secure medical supplies. From this experience the Red Cross came into being.

Within four years, Dunant had spread the story of his experience. Having seen the consequences of war firsthand and being someone who had always sought to serve others, he now asked himself what he could do to relieve suffering in future wars. He wanted to organize people for this cause. He traveled through Europe lecturing and meeting with government officials. He sought the support of well known people including the English writer Charles Dickens, the French writer Victor Hugo, and the founder of modern nursing, the Englishwoman Florence Nightingale. On October 26, 1863, thirty-nine delegates representing 15 countries assembled in Geneva to found an international war relief organization that they named the International Committee of the Red Cross.

They adopted as their symbol a red cross on a white background (a reversal of the colors on the Swiss flag) and drafted a treaty that guaranteed neutral status to relief workers on the battlefield. That treaty is still known by the name the Geneva Convention.

It would be years before Dunant was recognized for what he had stimulated, years of destitution, being disowned by family and shunned by friends. When it all ended, Dunant left most of his prize money to charities in Norway and Sweden. The rest went to the lodging house, where he had lived for almost 20 years, for the endowment of a free bed for the poor.

What struck me most about Dunant's story was the humanity. What makes us recoil when we experience firsthand inhumanity is often the stimulus for a quantum leap in personal evolution. Certainly this was the case when Betty Williams saw the explosion that left a wounded mother childless. The fact of her new realization, that such inhumanity was senseless and a waste, precipitated a new response – the mobilization of thousands, in hours, to march from the town to the cemetery where the children were buried.

Betty understood that the motivation for peace is needed to make any idea of peace work. *"Unlocking the desire for peace would never have been enough,"* she said. *"All the energy, all the determination to express an overwhelming demand for an end to the sickening cycle of useless violence would have reverberated briefly and despairingly among the people, as had happened so many times before ... if we had not organized ourselves to use that energy and that determination positively, once and for all."*[41]

Betty often talked of the reality of peace as hard work, emphasizing that the things in our world do not just happen, a sentiment spoken by Alva Myrdal, herself an advocate of women's and children's rights and winner of the 1982 Nobel Peace Prize.

In these days of building the world's first Peace Dome we possess a growing sense of bringing something precious into the world. As metaphysicians we realize that life is a combination of individual efforts and divine providence. Each person who experiences being at the right time at the right place with the right people has made a series of choices that led them there. Many would hear Dunant's story and think ill of him. "What bad luck!" they might say. "How horrible!" Yet how Dunant saw his experience, what he thought as a result of it, and how he shared it with others, continues to live through the organization he founded 140 years ago.

The truth is destiny can come to us at any time. We meet the love of our life. The opportunity of a lifetime comes our way. Everything just comes together for us. We describe it in many ways. Our lives are filled with moments of opportunity. The beauty is we each have every available opportunity to choose a productive, healthy, meaningful, and fulfilling existence, we need only choose to receive it. Many disavow this choice with perceived limitations and judgements. Each time my mind is tempted in that direction I remember Gandhi, Martin Luther King, and Nelson Mandela sitting for hours and sometimes weeks and years in a jail cell, their spirits never imprisoned, merely their bodies. This reminds me that thought is cause, and how I think about my life determines my capacity for goodness and that one person manifesting truth makes a profound difference in our world.

A universal moment of mindfulness is present in the story of each Nobel laureate. It is the moment that caused them to transcend the limits of humanity, reaching for answers with their reason. At the time we met – in March 2003 – the United States and Great Britain had invaded Iraq. This intention upon the part of our nation had been the subject of world debate for weeks, and now in spite of insufficient world support we were starting a war.

I shared with the group a letter (see next page) I had received just the day before from the director of our School in Des Moines, Iowa. Her words echo the thoughts of so many, as we stand united by telecommunications of all kinds, when senseless death halfway around the world enters into our living rooms, searing hearts and opening minds.

Karen's letter conveys the power of a unifying ideal and the fulfilment found in realizing your purpose in something greater than yourself. Like Betty Williams, Karen goes to work everyday. She is a divorced mother supporting two children. Her life is busy, filled with ends to meet. Like Betty, she has an inner desire to serve, to help, to make a difference and she has found a means to do so. For Betty it was the Peace People, for Karen it is directing a School of Metaphysics.

When we invite others into our lives, our sense of Self importance can quickly grow. Acts of kindness are always rewarded. People may forget our good deeds, ignore them or take them for granted, the Universe never does. There are infallible laws governing creation in our Universe. They function equally for us all whether young or old, king or pauper, scholar or workman. What sets them into motion, what causes them to work, is our thought.

There is an old question posed in many cultures that goes something like, "Where would you rather live, in Heaven with ten fools or in Hades with one wise man?" This is an amazing puzzle for the mind to conceive. It is an open door to elevated thinking in your life. There is no right or wrong answer, just the one you choose, for the reasons you see.

February 5, 2003

Dear Dr. Barbara,

I just listened to the Peace Dome Dedication tape at our area teacher's meeting. This is so well timed for me. My daughter called me Sunday afternoon just as the meeting was finishing. She could hardly talk because she was crying. She had just found out that a close friend of hers was being shipped over to the Middle East in preparation for the war (with Iraq). He is nineteen years old. She couldn't understand why there was still war in 2003. I didn't know what to say to her because I don't understand it either. I have always thought that things could be worked out or talked through to a resolution.

We talked for a while until she calmed down. I explained to her about the world's first Peace Dome being built and dedicated this fall on the campus of the College (of Metaphysics). I told her how it was located in the Midwest on the other side of the world from the Middle East, that it would balance the energies. I explained that we were inviting people from all over the world to come and visit and share this vision of world peace. I told her about the Universal Peace Covenant and that we would say it every day to help bring about peace. As I talked to her, I saw how important the Peace Dome is to the world. You are right. The Middle East receives a lot of the world's attention. It's time for the world to focus on something much more important.

I see the Dedication as a way to balance people's attention and direct it to something more positive. I can see the vision in the opening projection becoming real, "...people from all over the world, all nationalities, all religious backgrounds coming together for a common goal...." during the Dome Dedication. I can feel the energy that is moving right now and it's awesome. It's time for a change.

On the tape the students and you were talking about visions you have had. I want to tell you about mine. During the Atlantean weekend, I had a vision that concerned the School of Metaphysics. In it I saw darkness and out of the darkness I saw light, domes of light that represented each of the different schools. I saw people from all over the world turning and coming to the light. It was very exciting to realize that I'm involved in this. In this vision, I felt this steady rhythm that echoed over and over throughout the weekend, that the time is now, people are waking up to realizing that they want more answers, and we are here for this purpose, to aid and serve humanity. This weekend really helped me to connect with my purpose for being in the school at this time.

You know, Dr. Barbara, I have always felt that I needed to serve something bigger than myself and I didn't know where to look or who to trust. Thank you for this opportunity to help serve mankind. I am planning on being at the college the week before the dedication. I would like to be a tour guide if possible, but to tell you the truth, I am willing to serve in any capacity that you might need me.

Thank you. Sincerely,

Karen Mosby   Des Moines, Iowa

A thoughtful tale from the Congo tells of two childhood friends who were determined to remain close companions always. When they grew up, they each married and built their houses facing one another.

One day a trickster from the village decided to test their friendship. He dressed himself in a two-color cloak that was divided down the middle, white on the right side, black on the left, and carried a yellow gourd in his arms. As he walked down the middle of the lane between the two houses he whistled to call attention to himself. One friend glanced up from his work in the garden long enough to say hello. The other friend looked out his window to see where the song was coming from.

Later that day, while the two friends enjoyed the sunset together one said, "Did you see that man in the white cloak walking down the street at noontime?"

"No," replied the other, "I saw a stranger in a black cloak though."

"Black? It must have been a different fellow. The man I saw wore white."

"Perhaps. The man I saw was whistling."

"So was the man I saw!" said the first man. "And he carried a large yellow gourd."

"Ah, so did this man!" the second responded. "It must have been the same man dressed in black!"

"He wasn't dressed in black. He was dressed in white," replied the first man, now convinced they had seen the same man.

"I know what I saw," said the second man. "The cloak was black."

"You don't know anything," the first insisted. "It was white!"

"So, you think I am blind as well as stupid! I am neither. I know what I saw. It was black!"

"White!"

"Black!" "White!" "Black!"

The two men began to push each other and roll on the ground shouting, "Our friendship is over!" They stopped only when a pair of sandaled feet stepped very near them. Quickly they moved back and away. Looking up they could clearly see the trickster in front of them in his two-color cloak.

The two friends looked at the trickster, then at one another. "We have lived side by side all our lives like brothers. It is all your fault that we are fighting. You started a war between us!"

"Don't blame me for the battle," the trickster replied, "I did not make you fight. Both of you are wrong. Both of you are right. Yes, what each one said was true. You are fighting because you only looked at my cloak from your own point of view!"

We all have reasons for everything we do. Even those who harm others often do so with well defined reasons.

Destiny comes to us when we can see from many points of view. Henri Dunant saw from the perspective of those dying on a battlefield. Betty Williams saw from the perspective of a mother who lost her three children and a young man who caused the deaths. Karen Mosby saw from her daughter's perspective.

In each instance love was the stimulus for the greater awareness – Henri's love for his fellowman, Betty's love for life, Karen's love for her own child. Love is what neutralizes conflict enabling two seeming opposites to live in the same space and time. In such a flexible mind, peace grows easily and light radiates.

Science teaches us that everything in nature has a use, a purpose, a benefit.

Where illumination reigns everything has a purpose, a place. Peacemaking in large part is the openness to see from another point of view. The skill frees us within ourselves and between ourselves and others. Jesus' teaching to "come as little children" passes through my mind. Children are naturally open, we teach them to close with our oftentimes unintentional fears. The admonition "don't talk to strangers" is the origin of separating from others, denying our connectedness as spiritual beings. It leads to prejudice, mistrust, and sometimes cruelty. The phrase "sins of the father" takes on new meaning when we see the young amongst us imitating our ways. Too often we are unconscious about the example we are setting for others.

Gandhi was very conscious about his learning. His writings reveal the stages of his own growing awareness, often told through his life experiences. He is an example of using your life with purpose and on purpose for soul growth and spiritual progression.

Gandhi lived in South Africa after he earned his law degree. There he said he learned that one who would serve will not waste a thought upon his own comforts. What an elevated way to view purpose. Most of us think of purpose as our own benefit. Gandhi's experiences taught him not to be concerned about his own wants for they can be burdens. He learned to take only what he strictly needed and to leave the rest. This Gandhi found led to a calm mind free of anger even when you might be put out.

This realization was won through many experiences of abuse from those holding prejudices toward people of color. Gandhi tells a story of traveling in the first class section of a train on a business trip. A white male passenger insisted that he sit back in third class. He objected saying he had a ticket. The man refused to acknowledge this telling Gandhi to leave or he would have the police remove him.

Gandhi believed he had every right to stay there and so he refused to leave voluntarily.

The police came and escorted him off the train. His possessions, including his coat, remained on the train. It was bitter cold and the rail-road station where he was left was deserted. It was here that Gandhi's individual purpose was elevated to one serving a greater whole. Gandhi writes,

"It was not my own injury or humiliation that infuriated me, it was the much deeper cancer of man's inhumanity to man, the persecution of whole races because of the difference in skin color and belief." [42]

Decades later the Dalai Lama referred to Gandhi as his mentor. It is easy to see why when we study the lives and words of both men. In alignment with Buddhist teachings, the Dalai Lama speaks of all suffering being caused by ignorance. "People inflict pain on others in the selfish pursuit of their happiness or satisfaction. Yet true happiness comes from a sense of inner peace and contentment, which in turn must be achieved through the cultivation of altruism, of love and compassion and elimination of ignorance, selfishness and greed." [43] Clearly his ideas, like Gandhi's, reflect an elevated purpose.

The Dalai Lama often teaches that we, all human beings, are a global family. What happens in one part of the world affects all of us, be it positive or negative. Modern communications technology gives us knowledge of this sometimes, as with the events of 9/11, as it occurs. The Dalai Lama makes the point that even when events are miles away, they affect us personally. Certainly this is known by anyone who has been moved to support efforts to feed starving children in Eastern Africa, or who feels a sense of joy when a family is reunited after decades of separation. It is also felt when crops and livestock are contaminated and our own health threatened when a nuclear accident happens in another country or when people who cannot agree take up weapons to prove themselves right. His Holiness describes this quite thoughtfully when he says, *"Our own security is enhanced when peace breaks out between warring parties in other continents."*

Security is one of the great purposes in life. Often it is viewed as freedom from fear, I think of it as wisdom born from experience. We form our view of security early in life. We learn to embrace life with an open attitude of love, hope, and thanksgiving or we are taught to shy away from, to shut out, to look for reasons to resist. Mother Teresa is the most eloquent advocate of early influence and training. Although she did not marry and have children, she understood family in the most profound way for she cared for children and the dying every day of her life. The understanding her experiences brought her is reflected in what she has to say, and this particular passage which she spoke during her acceptance speech for the 1979 Nobel Peace Prize attests to the sense of purpose that is very strong when we are young.

"Some time ago in Calcutta we had great difficulty in getting sugar, and I don't know how the word got around to the children, and a little boy of four years old, Hindu boy, went home and told his parents: I will not eat sugar for three days, I will give my sugar to Mother Teresa for her children. After three days his father and mother brought him to our home. I had never met them before, and this little one could scarcely pronounce my name, but he knew exactly what he had come to do. He knew that he wanted to share his love." [44]

The lesson the little Hindu boy teaches is a universal one. We are indeed here to love one another. This is a simple truth. As we age other purposes seem to take importance. We want to be smart or popular or strong or courageous or honest or successful, and the imagination goes on. We become scattered in our thinking until we no longer remember why we are here.

When we remain steadfast in love, letting go of whatever doubt has taken root, we keep in our sights what each experience is for. By reaching for truth, our purposes become clear. All human experiences are for the purpose of learning about love. This is why the idea exists in every culture and religion around the world.

A Father's Love

I love my little boy Hezekiah. I also love Hezekiah's mommy who is my wife Barbara.

I love seeing Hezekiah at PeaceMakers. Most of the time he is running around having fun. "What!" you say. "How can a boy be running around during a meeting?"

PeaceMakers is a different kind of gathering. It is a wonderful place to study spiritual ideals. It is designed for children and adults. I have discovered that children learn best when in motion. Often we call this play. As children play, they exercise their imagination. At the same time they are absorbing vast amounts of information into the brain.

So PeaceMakers is a place for children to learn, not only about God but about themselves and others also.

Often Barbara Condron will lead the group in acting out a short story, a type of improvisation. This is very instructional for it provides everyone present with a whole experience. It also provides the children present with an opportunity to play while they are learning and every adult has a little bit of the child in them. Some more than others.

Hezekiah always enjoys these plays. Sometimes he participates as one of the characters in the improv. Other times he jumps up and down enjoying what he sees other people doing while enacting the story.

Because the stories chosen have a good thought, moral, or virtue, young Hezekiah also learns about right thinking and right action.

Sometimes we draw pictures describing the stories we tell. Hezekiah loves drawing and he is very good at it.

Since children learn best when they are at play, the children who attend PeaceMakers have an opportunity to learn and play.

Perhaps you may remember sitting in an adult meeting as a child for what seemed like hours as the lecture or sermon went on and on. Yet you may have loved arts and crafts and participatory learning where there were fun things to do. Every week PeaceMakers, held at the College of Metaphysics, provides this. Most people who attend have a fun time finding peace.

Often when acting out a play or story Kie is the one who will choose the actors and parts for a play. Every adult enjoys being picked by this child who is wise beyond his years. Then as the adults are acting out the story, Hezekiah happily engages in being a part of it in one form or another.

The important point I believe is that children be raised with the idea that they can participate in spiritual gatherings. They can participate in education, in schooling, whatever form it may take. They can participate in family life and community life. The child is taught that life is participatory and that each child and each adult has the freedom to do so, to experience the fullness of life.

Like so many souls now coming to Earth, our son is an exceptionally talented and gifted child. The keys to each child reaching their full potential is within the grasp of each of us. We must do whatever we can to foster their unfolding as enlightened souls. – Dr. Daniel Condron

As reasoning beings, our potential to learn is multiplied. When the foundation for reason is love, what man creates cooperates with the universe. There is no more senseless deforestation or thoughtless killing of people or animals.

The openness to learn is natural for spirit. You see it everyday in children. One child picks a flower and gives it to another to both their delights. One child paints a tree pink and another wants to try purple. One child introduces his friend to another friend.

Each child's world expands with each exchange, and growth is made possible.

Today we gave our minds time to dwell on the purpose of life. We contemplated love as purpose then we illustrated what our minds saw, and heard, and felt, tasted, and smelled. We could use images and/or words in any color, shape, form. Our inks were markers and our canvas, irregularly shaped watercolor paper roughly 3-4 inches in diameter. Each of us chose a piece, some looked like countries, others were polygons or ovals. No two were alike, as surely as no two drawings would be the same.

When we had completed our expressions of love, we found their place in the puzzle outline, a 24x36 sheet with the word "Love" written in calligraphy at an angle stretching from the lower left corner to the upper right corner. What we created together you can see below.

As the pieces went in, we marveled at what we had created individually and together. The power of love to unite was there before our eyes. The reality that when we create in love, we are in that moment connected with all of creation. Our pieces "fit". They were connected, not as if we had planned it out through conscious mind forethought, rather this connectedness arose from Universal Mind, that inner connection between all sentient, self-aware beings. Here before us was the representation of our place in the universe.

This was such a beautiful illustration of how, when we each strive to harmonize the inner and outer Self, we become attuned to each other and the universe itself. By cultivating the still, open mind we are free to learn, to understand, to grow, to fulfill our destiny, our purpose in life. We have an idea of where we fit into the great scheme of things. That is the security that comes from purpose.

A Chinese tale came to mind.

> *One day, Elephant came upon Hummingbird lying flat on its back on the ground. The bird's tiny feet were raised up into the air.*
>
> *"What on earth are you doing, Hummingbird?" asked Elephant.*
>
> *"I have heard the sky may fall today," replied Hummingbird. "If that should happen, I am ready to do my part in holding it up."*
>
> *The elephant was amused by the hummingbird's ambition and could not resist mocking the tiny bird. "Do you think those little feet can hold up the sky?"*
>
> *"Not alone," the little bird said, "but each must do what he can. And this is what I can do."*

We were talking about how our experiences are changing the way we see ourselves, the Peace Dome, and the world. In the summer of 2002 we had written the three-part chant we call *"Satyagraha"* during ... a PeaceMakers! Dr. Pam Blosser led the group that created the first movement which is a repetition of the words "Satyagraha, pravi! Pravi!" Subsequently, whenever we perform the chant, she initiates it, singing the same three words over and over again. This has had a profound affect on her consciousness.

"What is in my mind the most these days," she said, "is satyagraha because I sang that part of the chant over and over again. That's the part that I led. I knew there was a reason why I was singing that part. I needed to cause it to move through me so I could understand why it was the part I was singing.

"Satyagraha means 'holding onto truth' and pravi is welcoming it into yourself. Every time the word truth comes up, satyagraha is the image I have.

"The idea that I have in my mind right now is a steadiness. When you hold onto something it's a steadiness of something greater than yourself that can be like a foundation. Something very strong. I've also been working with the thought of power, drawing power into myself and what it is.

Satyagraha is along the same lines because truth is power.

"As we worked on *The Invitation* I wanted to memorize all the lines because I wanted to embody all of it into myself. Something that Tenzin said fit so perfectly for Paul. Something Mother Teresa said fit so perfectly for Erika and her learning. I could see it for every one of them. I wanted to be able to live lines, have them so much in my consciousness that I can live them. I knew this wasn't happening for me yet. I am experiencing desire, and longing for that kind of consciousness all the time.

"Now that I'm working on the annual *Thresholds* issue – it's all about the Peace Dome – I have the great privilege of living not only the Dome but the consciousness of so many people who have received and given because the Dome exists. I get to live with Erika sweeping the sacred chamber of the Dome and Matthew showing the upper level to the salesman who just stopped in on his way to somewhere else. Whatever people have said about what excites them about the Peace Dome, I get to live with on a daily basis. And I love it! I'm realizing my heart and all the energies above the heart are being activated. I get breathless and I can feel the energy moving.

"I want to understand what has caused the shift in my thinking because I had experiences with the Dome before, but this is constant. I think it is the idea of connecting with the planet in a viable, real sense. Since 9/11, I have prayed, 'May peace prevail on Earth' over and over. Perhaps that is part of it. The way I'm connecting with that prayer and the energy of the Dome can cause peace to prevail on Earth. It is going to happen."

When I heard Pam's words the thought that came into my mind was purpose. I knew after many years of seeking and finding, practicing and inspiring, she had found her purpose, her unique voice. She had found her love, her passion, and in time all the advantages of realization would follow.

Pam and I had just talked the day before about a call she made to Linda Twyman. Linda is the former wife of James Twyman, who was a School of Metaphysics student Pam taught years ago and who now is becoming quite well known worldwide as the Peace Troubadour. Linda said that in the early years James used to go to peace rallies and everyone was fighting, and he knew that wasn't what he was looking for. So he struck out on his own, spreading *his* message of peace everywhere he goes.

I could clearly see the connection between these two souls - Pam and James. Pam remembers James because she once taught him, influenced him, and there exists a parallel between them.

I remembered a story Pam told about a seminar she attended at the Parliament of the World's Religions in 1993 in Chicago. The topic was heartfelt peace but everyone was arguing, fighting over ideas of what it is. Pam was frustrated, disappointed, disheartened, and ultimately invigorated by the experience. She talked about it often, each time seeing a bit more, understanding a bit more of what heartfelt peace is. She was developing her vision, *her* message of inspirational peace.

I felt very certain in the moment, hearing Pam speak, that the Peace Dome and satyagraha is her message to give the world. They are the means for her to express her purpose for being here.

Sometimes we are born with a sense of purpose, like the Dalai Lama. Sometimes we seem to happen upon it, like Henry Dunant and Betty Williams. Sometimes we spend our lives preparing for it like Mother Teresa, Pam Blosser, and you.

Footnotes from *Lesson Eight*

41 Betty Williams, acceptance speech © The Nobel Foundation, 1967

42 Mohandas K. Gandhi, quoted in Gandhi, The Man

43 H.H. the Dalai Lama, acceptance speech © The Nobel Foundation, 1989

44 Mother Teresa, acceptance speech © The Nobel Foundation , 1979

What is friendship?

Kelly G.

Friendship is the <u>energy between</u> people
that is born from a <u>mutual desire to learn</u>
from one another. Friendship is <u>non judgemental</u>.
Friendship is the <u>trusting exchange</u> ability between folks
to <u>open</u> to one another & <u>communicate freely</u>.
Friendship exists so that we can see ourselves
through <u>someone else's eyes</u>. It is a caring type of <u>love</u> that
holds us then it is the <u>joy</u> & <u>support</u> of <u>growing together</u>
and watching another grow.

**Friendship is the trusting exchange that allows individuals
to grow and learn from one another.**

GIVING & RECEIVING —
The feeling of giving was akin to meeting someone for the first time — allowing
the first connection to be whole & completely trusting.
I was confident for the first time in my life to give of myself
& learned to do it without fear.
The feeling of receiving was more akin to the first
water of a shower. I was also open to simply be touched
by what I was given. I wanted to create a space
of openness & receptivity.

Jason Fry

Unconditional support & love with the goodness for all concerned.
The desire to see another succeed for pure & selfless reasons.
Friendship is ...
**Unconditional Truth Love & Support directed by the desire to see another succeed
for pure and selfless reasons.**
giving
I felt a release. that there was an abundance of what I had to give. I wanted to speak in the
first person instead of the third, saying "I am your friend. I give you Truth Love & Support.
I want you to succeed because it is your birthright to do so & my privilege
to aid you in any way I can.
Receiving
It was more an experience of Receiving the "person" then just their words.
I wanted to cry out in joy, to embrace them.
— and we did cry together
and embrace in mind & spirit as we
looked into each others eyes,
the window to the soul.

Lesson Nine

ACTIVITY

*"Somehow we must transform
the dynamics of the world power struggle
... to a positive contest*

*to harness man's creative genius
for the purpose of making peace and prosperity
a reality for all of the nations of the world."*

Natalie Axberg. Dallas.

The experience with giving was a very powerful feeling,
having a part of yourself to share and knowing you are
adding to someone.

Receiving was humbling, and also a very powerful feeling. I
experienced much more emotion personally on the receiving side.

Both experiences were very powerful, and I felt an incredible,
raw, soul connection.

What is Friendship?
Damian

Friendship is still. It is consistent. It runs deep
and cannot be thwarted. Friendship is divine joy in action.
Friendship is the willingness to look at self and others
again and again and again. Friendship, like surrender
is the evolution of giving. Friendship is also unconditional love
and the willingness to change.

Distilled Essence:
**Friendship is the evolution of giving, divine joy in action,
and the willingness to change.**

Giving — I experienced abundant joy and connectedness
while offering the truth with Love. I want this at all times.

Receiving — It was somewhat more difficult to receive,
although it was a wonderful experience to receive the mind,
heart, and words of all the others.

I send my Circle of Love

Through interaction we can learn so much faster. Think of it this way, you can teach yourself how to use a computer by reading a manual or you can have someone who knows more than you show you what they have learned how to do.

Which is faster?
More fun?
More enlightening?

Interaction allows us the opportunity for mutual growth. Where people communicate, understanding thrives. When an open mind meets a still mind, we learn about ourselves and each other.

It sounds so simple, how do we accomplish it? Is it any wonder that no matter how much people want peace, it eludes us?

Between two nations a refusal to interact leads to prejudice, conflict, and the threat of war. This was the experience of Americans and Russians following W.W. II. History calls it the cold war meaning it did not bring widespread death and destruction but the thought of it, the possibility of it, was always thick in the air.

In the early 1980's, when the world was at the mercy of these two superpowers — the United States and the United Soviet Socialist Republic — the two countries' leaders Ronald Reagan and Mikhail Gorbachev met. Later Reagan reminisced, *"I couldn't help but say to him (Gorbachev) (to) just think how easy his task and mine might be in these meetings....if suddenly there was a threat to this world from some other species, from another planet, outside the universe. We'd forget all the little local differences that we have between our countries, and we would find out, once and for all, that we really are all human beings here on this Earth together."*

It is a fact of human nature that the presence of a common enemy unites us. This is why we can so easily be mobilized to fear and make war upon others. Certainly people on one side can band together to fight the other. This kind of unity is its own reward, leaving separation, discord, and too often the animosity that fuels future wars. I am reminded of the attacks by terrorists on the World Trade Center in New York City in 2001.

Like most Americans I was deeply affected by the events of 9/11. I saw in real time the second plane fly into the second tower on television and in the hours of the following days I was moved into action. That action took on two forms worthy of merit that I want to share with you here.

One was to create the multidimensional experience called "Reconcile" which remains on our website at www.som.org (http://www.som.org/12MDLiving/911/wtc%20reconcile/titlepage.htm). Originally these steps were to help people put their thoughts and feelings about 9/11 into perspective. Now they function as a multidimensional guide for confronting any fear and doubt and transforming them into thoughtful, more enlightened actions. "Reconcile" remains available because the need for, and act of, reconciliation may arise and can occur any time in our lives.

The second action I took was to write a letter to the editor which I sent to several newspapers.

September 16, 2001

Dear Editor:

The drums of war echo in our collective consciousness. The undeniable spirit that wants to live and now fears being quieted.

If we must wage war, let it be a war on ignorance. On the refusal to believe what life unfolds before us, for the betterment of our souls, for the unification of our spirit.

Blessings are everywhere. Our media reflect them back to us through firemen, and policemen, and friends, and spouses, and children. The omnipresent recognition of need and immediate response to fill it. So often we call it the American spirit, one that continues giving, and giving, and giving. At some point we must wonder, what is the blessing of our nation? The blessing we have in common.

Must we be destined for more death and destruction, that acts guided by fear and retribution will certainly breed? Some speak of the psychological impact of the past few days while missing the truths that are universal. All of us find our beliefs being tested, for these are the same growing pains of every child as he reaches to expand his world. We must face these pains, knowing they will pass. If we are open to self examination we can find the causes and cures thus ensuring an individual and national healing.

Even as we are given the facts of what happened, we still grapple with disbelief, finding it difficult to accept what is entering into our consciousness. Like an invading virus that gives a death sentence to the body, our instinct is to survive. And so instinctually we push away anything that might threaten the underpinning beliefs of our lives.

Yet the nature of life is forward motion, growth, change. Dr. Elizabeth Kubler-Ross identified it years ago as the five stages of death. The denial of disbelief in time gives way to the anger of helplessness and the clutching for power. The extremes of bargaining follow, paving the way for the depression that precedes acceptance. At the School of Metaphysics we know these as the five stages of fighting change. Any change.

The way to stop fighting is to surrender, not as in "give up" but as the acceptance of who we are and what we are within a situation we have caused. Almost everyone who has spoken has affirmed the belief that something good will come from all this. It is time we transformed that belief into the firm resolve of knowing. Now, more and more of us, want to know the good. We can, as we reach to know the aftermath of ceasing the constant struggle that results from fighting change.

So how can we know? Many will tell us we are not meant to know these things. But the heart that reasons knows better. This is living, breathing visualization - human being as creator. This is our destiny as thinkers.

I have been in positions of leadership all my life, dedicating my adult years to teaching people to be whole, functioning selves - leaders of self and others. I understand the magnitude facing political leaders, clergy, business executives, educators, parents, when those in their charge, those whose trust is placed in them, ask "Why?"

Almost everyone who has spoken has affirmed the belief that something good will come from all this. It is time we transformed that belief into the firm resolve of knowing.

The United States was built by visionaries - those who imagined a better life and were willing to assume responsibility for freedom. The United States is still built by visionaries, and it is time for us to imagine what this ideal means today. For a nation, the responsibility for freedom is individuals, each unique, sharing a common ideal, a common hope, a common language, as well as a common land. There is much we can do to further live this ideal. And leadership in all sectors of life is essential.

What would happen if President Bush came forward saying what I have heard at least a few common people say in these past few days. What if our President said, "With over eight million people, New York City is the 14th largest city in the world. The family and friends of the people killed were self-described Italians, Czechs, Vietnamese, African-Americans, Iranians, Israelis, Chinese, Irish. These were citizens from around the globe, living, working, and playing together on a few acres of land. They represented what can happen in all the lands of our world. And because of that, what happened to them on September 11th, happened to every person on Earth."

New York has always prided itself on being a microcosm of our world. The living example of a melting pot of cultures, ideas, religions, of human beings and in these past days it has proven its mettle.

The WTC bombing was an act of terrorism on the reality of the ideal that all people on this planet can live together in peace. This was not an attack on the U.S., as so much of world media would lead us to believe. This was an act of terrorism on all of the world.

All great masters of consciousness have known we are all the same human beings. In the last century Mohandas K. Gandhi in India, Martin Luther King in the U.S., and Nelson Mandela in South Africa embodied the vision of one race, the human race moving into a more enlightened, a more spiritually uplifted awareness of self and others.

Who will be the first to do so in the 21st century?

From the ashes of September 11, 2001 a challenge for this century rises like a giant phoenix. The United States was built by visionaries - those who imagined a better life and were willing to assume responsibility for freedom. The United States is still built by visionaries, and it is time for us to imagine what this ideal means today.

The *Universal Peace Covenant* says, *"We call upon each individual to create and foster a personal vision for peace."* For the ideal to be personal, for it to have meaning in your life, it must have purpose. When it does, it is easier to conduct ourselves with the goodness for all concerned. It is easier to know what is right, and to do it.

Leadership is a universal element in the Nobel laureates' lives. They used their lives, their time on this planet, to interact with others inspiring them to be more, know more, do more. Mother Teresa founded the Sisters of Charity; Martin Luther King, the Southern Christian Leadership Conference; Betty Williams and Mairead Corrigan, Peace People; Albert Schweitzer, a hospital in French Equatorial Africa; Linus Pauling, led the U.S. ban on nuclear weapons testing and wrote much of the treaty signed by the U.S. and Russia; and the Dalai Lama has been the leader of the Tibetans since age 2.

Their lives attest to vision – the power of imagination employed to unite toward a common goal. This is such a significant step beyond the kind of unity that a common enemy provides. We have the capacity to be better, to do more. To do unto others as we would have them do unto us. The opening of the heart and the elevation of consciousness are the hope of humanity.

The work of peace

Our values were sorely tested in March of 2003. There were so many ironies in our lives. Here was our community, three quarters of the way through a journey that would culminate in dedicating the world's first Peace Dome in seven months. We had been living what you have read here for weeks, and now the country we live in was moving toward leading a war on a small nation in the cradle of civilization, Iraq, without the sanction or support of the vast majority of our world's governments.

I could conceptualize the dilemma so easily by envisioning circles within circles within circles. The first circle is the self, then the community, followed by the nation, then the world, the global community. The reality that these outer communities were not in harmony had to affect our own individuality, and one of the mental tools every metaphysician has is Self respect, the willingness to look at Self again, again, and again from different viewpoints – and learn. This PeaceMakers we would do the work of peace.

The experience was polarizing for people throughout the world. Whatever goodwill September 11th may have seeded was quickly uprooted in a global argument about how to respond to a country who repeatedly refused to play by the rules. Missed deadlines and finally war was splashed in newspaper headlines every day. This day we talked about Alva Myrdal.

Alva entered our lives as a result of wanting to make a place for Dr. Pam Blosser in *The Invitation*, a theatrical experience that was blossoming from our PeaceMaker's gatherings. As I skimmed through a book on the laureates I was struck by Alva's picture. She looked a bit like Dr. Pam, and when I read about her, absolutely, she was the one!

Alva was from Sweden. Early on she was an advocate for children and women, founding a school to train teachers of children, then serving in the legislature where she helped form Sweden's welfare state. Dr. Pam, who studied Maria Montessori's work in the '70's in England, is director of our summer camp for children and was serving a term as President of the School of Metaphysics.

Alva was the first female to head a department of the United Nations. She left that post to become Sweden's ambassador to India. Dr. Pam had been among the leadership of the first People to People delegation of metaphysicians to India in 1999.

In the 1960's, as head of Sweden's delegation to the UN disarmament conference in Geneva, Alva's knowledge and passion for nuclear disarmament grew shaping the remainder of her life, as most assuredly is Dr. Pam's knowledge and passion for peace. For these reasons Alva had much to give to Dr. Pam and Dr. Pam could bring much to Alva in how she would embody her.

Alva Myrdal belonged to the world community. As a researcher and disarmament expert, with a wide knowledge of the problems of world politics, she commanded attention in the international forum, and not least in her literary work where her influence was substantial.

The beauty of Alva Myrdal is her willingness to identify just what thoughts and activities are. When she was alive, Alva became a rallying point for men and women who believe that mind will triumph over matter.

Her command of this shines throughout her speech accepting the Nobel Peace Prize in 1982.

For instance, she described arms as *"tools in the service of rival nations, pointing at the possibility of a future war."* She went on to say that preparations for war and warring itself have acquired a type of legitimacy. The escalating production and export of arms made them available more or less to anyone, right down to handguns and stilettoes. Mrs. Myrdal describes her ideas brilliantly.

"The age in which we live can only be characterized as one of barbarism. Our civilization is in the process not only of being militarized, but also being brutalized. There are two main features which mark this senseless trend. Let me briefly - just as everything in my lecture must necessarily be abbreviated and simplified - refer to them as rivalry and violence.

Rivalry for the power to exploit the headlong on-rush of technology militates against cooperation. The result is increased violence, with more and more sophisticated weapons being used. This is precisely what sets out our age as one of barbarism and brutalization. But the moment of truth should now have arrived." [45]

Her speech is clear, concise, thoughtful, and potentially polarizing. The tendency to want to agree or disagree with Alva actually lessens the value of what she offers, for in her highly educated way she insists that we think about things that we take for granted. She insists that we determine what our values are, and determining values is what purpose is all about. When we value someone or something we treat them accordingly. Our thought dictates our action.

The box that an appliance comes in is carelessly tossed away by the person who wants to use the new stove or refrigerator. To the happy child who finds it, the box can become a new house, a spaceship, or a musical instrument. "One man's refuse is another man's treasure."

Such is the nature of physical existence. Hindus call it the pairs of opposites, life's inherent ironies and paradoxes. At what moment does a good become bad? When is enough food too much food? A helping hand, a harmful one? Answering these questions creates the balance in life.

Our President had sent our country into war which sent us grappling with the pairs of opposites. Was the war the right thing to do? When was killing others ever right? Should offenders be punished? If they are allowed to go free what will that inspire in others who would like to try? What is sacrifice to a cause? When is it worth it? When do you stop talking? Waiting? Hoping?

These were the kinds of questions we were starting to ask ourselves, and it was causing considerable overturning of long-held beliefs. Values were being tested and lives were being changed, thousands of miles from the scene of battle, here where the Peace Dome lives.

Because we practice mental disciplines, such as concentration and meditation, we daily cultivate peace as a state of mind. Experiences with calmness, love, light, and bliss teach you what peace is. Ideas that peace is the opposite of or absence of war fall away.

Our desire to live peaceably begins by thinking peacefully. Here, at the College community we want to love one another. We want to do more than just get along, we want to support one another, to work together for the common good. This is our everyday effort and it shows as we build the Peace Dome.

Being citizens of the United States, our country's warring actions affected our consciousness. One of the thoughts this action brought forth in my thinking centered on old ideas of good and bad I was taught as a child. I used to be very grateful that there were people who were willing to go and do "dirty work". I had been taught by my Christian family that killing was a sin, a crime against God. At the same time I was taught that communism was godless and that communists would try to take away my God if my country allowed it. The end result was the idea that were the communists to invade our country, we would lose our freedoms, one of which is the freedom to worship as we choose. With this ruling thought, defending our country then became a necessary evil, and there had to be those willing to do the work.

This line of logic operated in my thinking – unconsciously – for years waiting for the power of reasoning to bring enlightenment.

In 2003, at the age of 50, this train of thought was surfacing to the light of a new understanding. This was thanks in part to Jimmy Carter's words, *"War may be a necessary evil, but it is always an evil."* How simple the truth is. How easy to overlook.

I had been taught to believe there are some people in the world who are inherently evil. The rationale follows that these are the ones you have to do the dirty work with. Something has to be done about them or they will hurt other people. This was the same line of thinking, the same collective unconscious thought that our President was using to justify invading another country.

As a child, I trusted the adults around me who fed and clothed me, who loved me. I believed them. As an adult thinker striving for wisdom, I could examine the thinking through the light of many life experiences, my own and that of others'. What I saw was fear. Where fear rules there is no peace.

I used to believe in an emotional way, what I believed to be a real way, that there were some people out to get me if given half a chance. From the well-intentioned but misguided "don't talk to strangers" of childhood to the "get it while you can" thinking, fear rules too many lives. Franklin D. Roosevelt's revelation back in 1930 that *"the only fear we have to fear is fear itself"* is timeless.

I have found that when I have a vision, an ideal, I am fearless. I have seen this in others. When the unexpected hero says he just did what he had to do, that it didn't take courage, I understand what he means. Such grasp of truth is the beginning of going beyond good and evil. Since this war with the Biblical Babylon, I no longer believe in evil.

The truth is as people learn to conduct themselves with a higher purpose in mind, Self government will make the need for external government obsolete. This is more than a lofty utopian ideal. It is a way of living a life that is worth living.

I am coming to realize the neither-either, yet both, in all my thoughts. Eastern Holy Scriptures call this process equanimity. In Western holy scriptures including the *Torah*, the Bible and the Koran, it is known as grace.

Today's PeaceMakers would be an exercise in equanimity, balance in each action. To examine our consciousness, we began by considering a question: "What is the war with Iraq revealing to me about the pairs of opposites?" We spent the first twenty minutes or so writing our answers, then we shared them. Our answers reflected our individual and collective search for equanimity. Now we share them with you in the hope that they will stimulate new awarenesses and bring you peace.

"Militarization proceeds not only through acts of war and the purchase of arms. It is also promoted - primarily, of course, where young men are concerned - by military training, defense manuals etc. Exercises and war games erode the basic ethical values contained in the command 'thou shalt not kill'. We tolerate, in fact, more and more the exact opposite of what both religious creeds and the international law on more humane warfare are endeavoring to instil in us."– Alva Myrdal [46]

John Harrison wrote:

"I am amazed to see people who either support or are against the war. There are many people who want or are being patriotic and supporting our troops and country even if they don't agree with the war. They seem to have forgotten the lessons of World War II where German people supported their country, troops and government right or wrong. The people wanting war (George Bush) can do so because 1) He won't be on the front lines getting maimed or killed, and 2) He probably doesn't have any children who will be out there either.

"The people for peace do so because they have lost loved ones in previous wars that accomplished little or nothing, religious beliefs, or other reasons. A lot of the world opinion is against our going to war but not for what will cause peace. Gandhi said non-violence would have worked against Hitler, but not without a lot of pain and suffering.

"I am mostly against the war with Iraq this time. I was in favor of getting rid of Saddam the first time during the Gulf War. Now I feel George W. Bush is lying to us to get rid of Saddam for his own personal reasons. He first said Saddam was involved in terrorism. He probably is but George Bush didn't supply the promised proof. His next excuse was Saddam Husein had weapons of mass destruction that threatened our national security. They still haven't found any. World opinion is against the U.S. fighting Iraq. It gives the appearance of us picking on weaker Arab countries only. I was thinking he would go after Libya next but North Korea is trying to get his attention.

"The final thought is how much will this end up costing us in lives, money, good will and other intangibles. What karma are we creating that we will reap? 2012 is not that far off or the tribulation. Are we becoming the anti-Christ?".

"The driving force in the development of our civilization, at least since the Renaissance, has evidently been the progress of technology. But technology is two-edged. It can always be exploited either by good forces or by evil forces. And we human beings do not seem to have succeeded to make a choice quite consciously, nor how to steer the considerable consequences." – A. Myrdal 47

Erika Scholz wrote....
"I was thinking about the need for greater understanding of the pairs of opposites. As a child I lived with the threat of the USSR and communism being the great evil against the American way. Since the fall of the Soviet Union I have watched other "evils" rise and fall around the world. For anyone with eyes to see, it becomes increasingly clear that the threat doesn't come from the evil of the day, but from ourselves. This is the beginning of the understanding of the pairs of opposites.

    "I myself have striven to understand my own need to have a common enemy in order to lead and unite people. It is the same among nations. The time is dawning where people begin to look within, when common creation is more compelling than common enemy. It starts here and now. If I expect to live in a community, a city, a nation, a world of peace I must first create the nations of peace within.

    "I'm not very connected with what's happening with the war. I don't read newspapers, I don't receive e-mails, I'm not talking to people except for what goes on here. I have almost no contacts, so I don't feel very, I know what's happening but I'm not—. If I was watching it on T.V. and hearing it a lot I'd probably have a lot of feelings about it.

    "I'm tired of war. I came into this world thinking war was ridiculous. I still think it's ridiculous and I don't know what else to do except focus on what I can do within myself to make those things that breed war in nations — to remove that from within myself. I don't know how to balance it. I've really tried my whole life. I mean I remember being younger than (8-year-old) Hezekiah, not getting it and being frustrated by it and thinking it seemed like a childish way to handle something. I would watch nations make threats and it just seemed like grown ups were acting like children. That they couldn't even solve problems as well as children could with the choices that nations made about things and I still feel about that."•

"A cultural factor promoting violence which nowadays undoubtedly is highly effective is the mass media. And particularly everything that enters our minds through pictorial media. A wide range of investigations on this subject have been made and published in many countries. Some programs tend to have a more momentary effect, while others confirm more permanent effects of indoctrination.

"The violence shown in the mass media also has a differentiated effect, since violence committed by the 'good guys' is imprinted more deeply in our apperceptions than violence committed by the 'bad guys'." [48]

Laurie Biswell's thoughts....

"Blame. Success - Failure. Commitment - Broken promises. Trust - Fear. I can see where both sides are standing for what the other side wants to change or sees as evil. Iraq sees us as materialistic. We see them as barbaric.

"Everyday American citizens pass by other American citizens laying on the streets. Theirs is the same thing we accuse the dictatorship of doing to his people. The only difference is we hide ours. We give examples to our children of selfishness and greed. Need to have the better house/car. Kid needs better toy/bike. Continues on and on, generation after generation. If we all look behind the physical we can see where the world peace begins. World peace begins within ourselves.

"Examining my childhood and watching other children notice how at a young age 'war games' are played out. Sword fighting. Balloon fights. 'Guns.' These are the way we understand the energies around us. Innocent then as we continue becoming more detriment.

"I believe this is a way we are striving to understand good - bad, right - wrong, good - evil, black - white. We want to play both sides and usually end up liking the dark side more. That's the exciting part. I think it was our way of trying to understand it. I wonder why? Why do you always want to play the villain with the dark hat? I think that's the ones you saw taking that action part. If you didn't have the guys in the black hats you wouldn't need the guys in the white hats to come to the rescue. One day we will no longer discover our separations as well as our connections. It's like where everything is together, both sides of the coin. Neither either yet both."•

"May I at this juncture make a personal confession? I have always regarded global development as a struggle between the forces of good and evil. Not to be simplified as a struggle between Jesus and Satan, since I do not consider that the process is restricted to our own sphere of culture. Rather perhaps to be symbolized in the most general terms as a struggle between Ormuzd, the good, and Ahriman, the evil. My personal philosophy of life is one of ethics.

"It seems to me as if the evil forces have now concentrated more and more power in their hands, Dare we believe that the leaders of the world's great nations will wake up, will see the precipice towards which they are heading and change direction?" –Alva Myrdal [49]

Pam Blosser: "I had a mixture of thoughts here. Us and them. We are "them" to much of the world. We think we are the good guys going in to save the world, Iraqi people, and ourselves from the bully evil. We the super power/the bully are fighting a third world country.

The idea of freeing the Iraqi people of totalitarianism is noble. How much have we been the bad guy supporting Israel and other leaders who encourage violence in these areas.

The war has stimulated all kinds of questions. Was the war absolutely necessary? We have killed thousands of Iraqi civilians and military, and wrecked their country, their economic and moral stability. It seems like taking a stick of dynamite to kill a fly.

After September 11 we did very few self respect lessons of why terrorists would want to destroy or hurt us. We were more polarized. Since we were the victims we became the good guys. Our answer was to fight back leading to invading Afghanistan — tit for tat — an eye for an eye and a tooth for a tooth. In our world that still thinks on a more human level this was a viable answer and one that could be understood.

The lines of good and evil are not as clear cut as they were. What appears to be a bad thing can have at its essence purging and healing. And what seems quite harmless (the way people dress, talk or what they watch on T.V., etc.) can have far reaching ill effects.

I don't know if I'm in a Libra phase or what because I go back and forth. I have a strong belief that everything in its essence is good. And war can have a good, and I think it's the way people use them that makes them good or evil in and of themselves. Just because we can make something good out of something that's not so good does that justify it or excuse why it was started in the first place?"•

"A point was reached long ago at which both the United States and the Soviet Union had such monstrous arsenals that further accretions became senseless. These have been 37 years of lunacy, of idiots racing against imbeciles, of civilized nations staggering blindly toward a finishing line of unspeakable peril." – Washington Post of April 13, 1982 [50]

Chris Madar's thoughts ...."For me it started on September 11th when my beliefs were tested — belief that America was safe, belief that people value life in the same way as me. There were rumors of terrorist factions in Columbia, Missouri, and the imagined possibility of chemical attacks.

　　　"I remember driving across Illinois and a small plane flying over and feeling anxious. I did a lot of self counseling on that drive. Did I want to live in these new fears or be free to move through the world with the ease of a mind that is still and centered?

　　　"What do I think and feel about Iraq? I have thought at times that we need to do this based on where humanity is as a whole. This is the way to protect ourselves from one another. This is always a temporary 'solution.' I have gravely disagreed with the thoughts and actions of our government, and questioned my own judgement because this was a group of people I believed in based on what I knew about them.

　　　"Recently my thoughts have dwelled on the experience of the people directly involved. I felt the fear and anxiety of the people in Iraq when I gave them my attention. What about the soldiers who have invaded and their experience? I've heard they've been given drugs. I believe their physical limits have been tested with food, water, and sleep. Are the lifelong repercussions of the self-induced pain worth it? Right now I think we've dug ourselves a deeper hole and betrayed the original intentions of our country.

　　　"I have learned beyond doubt that peace begins within ourselves, I witness the start of world wars by paying attention to my thoughts and feelings and watching how those I live with live with each other. I am more aware of the truth *thought is cause* in everything.

　　　"I just saw things differently than I ever had before with the benefit of all the reporters over there because it's giving people, some people at least, a chance to tell their stories right then. And I know the benefit of talking, and that kind of story being shared will open doors for the others that I think in the past, the veterans just closed them. And they did live with it their whole life. I never realized that this might be a way for them to process it. It's a part of their life but it isn't where they get stuck in their life. And that may be why all those reporters are over there."•

Having journalism in my background, I could see Christine's point. This is reality media of a different kind. I was a bit young when television first brought the Viet Nam war into our living rooms but I remember those older talking about it for years. When pictures of death were telecast hours after the event, my mother would turn off the set or leave the room. In the 21st century, we experience this dark side of humanity in real time.

This I predict that when "good guys" come home from war, saying, "It was terrible. It's ugly. You don't ever want to do this." Ideas of war as a viable option are going to change.

I have awakened to the truths Alva articulates so well since the soul we call Hezekiah came into our lives. Now an eight-year-old mystic child, he is a constant source of learning, insight, and stimulation for me on every level. For instance, it was only when I had the responsibility of raising a son that I became aware of collective thoughts about boys and about girls. I had not noticed before how humanity preys upon its young males to prove themselves.

For example, most fathers are proud the first time their sons get a black eye. "Well, what's the other guy look like?" the father asks. They joke to cover the hurt or embarrassment. This teaches a misplacement of the ego, a distortion of perception that will follow the boy throughout his life. If the boy does nothing to retaliate, he quickly learns this is unacceptable when he is labeled a sissy, which teaches him to devalue women at the same time it encourages him that "a man" strikes back. This thinking leads to war whether in a schoolyard, a business, or a battlefield.

Females unconsciously further the conditioning by actively expecting the male to win them over other suitors and then protect them against imagined harm. How many duels have been fought to protect a woman's honor? How many wars have been fought as revenge for deeds claimed by women? Whose face launched a thousand ships? Betty Williams understood women's role in either promoting peace or undermining it.

From girlfriends to sports coaches, a high percentage of the people in the United States unconsciously encourage our boys to become bullies. As Alva says, *"It does not just happen."* Good versus evil is everywhere in our media. From popular cartoons to classic fairy tales to the evening news, the nervous system for our planet – multimedia – continuously feeds back to us that we have reason to be afraid.

Martin Luther King said that our experience should tell us that war is obsolete. *"If we assume that life is worth living and that man has a right to survive, then we must find an alternative to war."* A purposeful man, King did not stop with this lofty concept. He described what action needed to be taken to build a peaceful world. He said it is necessary to love peace and sacrifice for it.

King sometimes told the story of Ulysses and the Sirens to illustrate this point. In this story and his stirring insights into its modern day application, King ignites the sense of elevated purpose in us all. He takes the mundane and makes it transcendent.

First the Greek story.

The Sirens had such an enticing song that sailors could not resist steering toward their island, thus perishing upon the rocks. Many men were lured to their death. They forgot home, duty, and honor as they flung themselves into the sea to be embraced by arms that drew them down to death. Ulysses was determined not to be lured by the Sirens. First he decided to tie himself tightly to the mast of his boat so when the Sirens called he could not go to them. His crew stuffed their ears with wax so they would not even hear the song.

Eventually Ulysses and his crew learned a better way to save themselves. They took on board the beautiful singer Orpheus whose melodies were sweeter than the music of the Sirens. When Orpheus sang no one bothered to listen to the Sirens. In a stirring metaphor, King likens the quest for peace to Orpheus' song:

"So we must fix our vision not merely on the negative expulsion of war, but upon the positive affirmation of peace. We must see that peace represents a sweeter music, a cosmic melody that is far superior to the discords of war. Somehow we must transform the dynamics of the world power struggle from the negative nuclear arms race which no one can win to a positive contest to harness man's creative genius for the purpose of making peace and prosperity a reality for all of the nations of the world.

"In short, we must shift the arms race into a 'peace race'. If we have the will and determination to mount such a peace offensive, we will unlock hitherto tightly sealed doors of hope and transform our imminent cosmic elegy into a psalm of creative fulfillment." [51]

"In this new popular movement of protest against nuclear weap-ons, women and, more and more churches and professional organi-zations are playing a leading role......in all sincerity, I personally believe that those who are leaders with political power over the world will be forced some day, sooner or later, to give way to common sense and the will of the people." –Alva Myrdal [52]

Dr. Daniel Condron's thoughts about....

"Opposites - War in Iraq

destroy - create
add to - tear down
end of regime - beginning of new government
good - bad
right - wrong
life - death
truth - lies
east - west
fossil fuels - alternative fuels
dictator - republic
freedom of religion - state of religion
Islam - Christianity/Paulinity
Old - new
ancient civilization - modern civilization
dry - wet
arid - humid
freedoms - restrictions

That's what I wrote about the pairs of opposites and the war in Iraq."•

Dr. Daniel Condron's words are descriptively succinct. Such words shed light on the situation at hand. This is the benefit of a still mind, a characteristic of the chancellor of the College of Metaphysics.

I remember Dr. Dan describing his response following 9/11. When asked what he gave after the collapse of the World Trade Center, he replied, "I gave my still mind." I remember when I heard him say this I felt a twinge of guilt that my mind was called into action – receiving information, studying it, reflecting, praying, meditating, creating. The charge produced by my guilt was neutralized through hearing people talk about their thoughts/feelings, and through leading them through the Reconcile experience. This freed me to appreciate Daniel's still mind.

To imagine my first response as a still mind was an amazing thought for me, one I would contemplate more often. My natural inclination was to reach out, to comfort, to help. To think being present is all that is necessary seems so simple to me. Before this time, I deemed it too simple, too easy, and in that I devalued it. I held being present in lesser esteem than action.

Dr. Dan's 9/11 still mind experience was my beginning of reevaluating each individual's worth as a healing presence. This is a concept we teach those who receive psi counseling training. As a counselor you don't have to know all the answers nor do you need to fix people. You do want to know what mental and spiritual resources are available to the person that will aid them to produce what they desire. Our experiences today with Alva illuminated several.

We ended this PeaceMakers with a stillpoint focus exercise. On the same piece of paper where we had written our thoughts, we drew a circle. Next, we placed a dot in the very center. For ten minutes we practiced an exercise in equanimity. Beginning with the dot, we focused our attention on that single point. Our gaze took in the entire circle with the mental attention remaining fixed in the center. That point became the doorway to the still mind.

After the exercise I looked at each person there, mentally embracing each one. A thought came back to me from a PeaceMakers a few weeks before when we explored love through a Spiritual Chakra, the dual circles like the one on friendship described throughout this book. I remembered the love I had given and received.

The thought I gave was

"Love is the need and the fulfillment of God."

The image I had received:

"Love is the breath throughout Creation."

As these thoughts came back to me, another memory surfaced. A small porcelain nick-nack on a living room table came into my mind. It belonged to my grandmother who was religiously devoted. The trinket was in the shape of an open book, a rose on the left and on the right, the words "God is love" were painted in gold leaf. Mentally I smiled and gave a pleased sigh of musing. God *is* love. I knew anew what it meant.

This experience today, of sorting out thoughts of war and good versus evil, was bringing several old memories into present time to be cleansed and made healthier for present-day use.

As we moved to form the circle of hands that enables us to become a force for love and light during our Circle of Love, another thought surfaced. This one was most profound for me. It was as if the heavens parted and the Creator spoke. *"God ... is .... practice,"* the voice said.

God is practice! What a concept! After decades of practice at speaking, writing, learning, teaching, breathing, listening, entraining consciousness, and so forth I realized I had yet to merge my images of practice with my image of God.

Until today.

Today I could admit there was quite a bit of negativity attached to how I had learned my ideas of practice. Practice did make perfect, yet in getting there sometimes practice was tiring, hard, boring, even embarrassing, a necessary evil in my young sometimes often conflicted life.

Still, as a child I learned the benefits of doing something again and again until you get it "right" and those showed in my life in physical monikers like test scores and later in paychecks.

As a young student in metaphysics in the 1970's, I upgraded my opinion of practice. Early on I formed very conscious, positive images of what practice means – increased concentration, deeper thinking, greater intimacy with self and others, Self mastery! I loved learning and growth. I loved repeating a lecture or poster several times, seeing change and improvement with each successive experience. I loved starting new classes, introducing people to the School and what it teaches. I even loved to learn the hard times when unwanted emotional reactions would come to the surface for my evaluation.

Over the years I had come to love life without the benefit of realizing how much I had fallen in love with practice!

Here it was, crystal clear in my mind today:

God is practice.

And love was the energizing catalyst that made it all happen. The residue of false beliefs about practice – fears of laziness or what others think or expect or thoughts of self doubt – was disappearing like sand through my fingers.

My thoughts were being reconstructed by that incredibly intelligent power that is our ability to mentally create, – again and again.

How many times is enough to hug a baby, watch a sunset, or to hear well-earned praise? I now understood the answer to that question.

Footnotes from *Lesson Nine*

45-49 Alva Myrdal© The Nobel Foundation, 1982

50 © *Washington Post*, 1982 [April 13, 1982]

51 Martin Luther King © The Nobel Foundation, 1964

52 Alva Myrdal © The Nobel Foundation, 1982

What is friendship
Ivy Norris

Friendship is connectedness. It is the willingness to move
and breathe with another through the different cycles
of life's experiences. It is holding an image of Their light (a vision),
honoring / supporting their process, towards this. It is giving and receiving
completely of love and truth to best ability.

**Friendship is connectedness with truth and a willingness to give completely
to them from this place.**

I really enjoyed the giving part, receiving I found was more difficult —
yet it was so precious to do — to see sweet faces coming around and
sharing their heart — it was a manifestation of what I believe
friendship to be.

Erika Scholz

Friendship
Warm water
inviting to sink into its caress
Cool forest
timeless boughs shelter in peace.
Deep night
endless, in tender mystery
Gentle dawn
awakens my soul's slumber
Brilliant day
You spark my spirit.

Warm & inviting, deep and timeless, it awakens my soul into a brilliant new day.
Giving
My heart was open. I felt like my thoughts were gifts I gave to another.
I felt like I embodied love.
receiving
My mind was still. My attention was on receiving the other person
fully into myself. I had thoughts at times that I was too full
& couldn't receive anymore. I stilled my mind & opened my
heart & was able to continue receiving.

Lessons Learned from the great
PeaceMakers

Candice (Columbia SOM)
Friendship is the reciprocity of love and respect.
It is the giving and receiving of positive energies.
Friendship is sharing with others one's thoughts, beliefs, opinions and ideas. It is trust — trusting that the other will not betray you and will be there for you when you need them, and being there for another when they need you. Friendship is the manifestation, the expression of love. Friendship is also transient. It is the meeting of two or more souls for the time when they need each other most. It can also be perpetual or enduring, it can last a lifetime or longer. Friendship is universal, and withstands the perceived limitations of time and space. It exists whether or not we still desire for it to be. It exists when our friends have come and gone, it exists when we are no longer "friends." **Friendship is the portrayal of humanity at its best.**

Everyone knows what friendship is, yet everyone expresses its meaning differently. Either expressed intellectually or emotionally, its meaning is still the same, yet friendship cannot be intellectualized. It was difficult to me to make and maintain eye contact as I was giving my expression of friendship. It was also difficult for me to receive everyone else's. It was difficult for me to express my own idea of friendship after I heard the many other ideas around me. I began to feel that my idea was in some way inferior, almost as if I didn't want to be here.

What is Friendship?
Kristen Carl
Closeness, honesty, Trust.
Friendship is when people can communicate to each other their deepest thoughts, and listen to each other with their hearts.
Through no judgements or criticism. Just listening with your heart, mind, and soul. Friendship can show up anywhere, friendship is giving and receiving.
Friendship is how the web of consciousness is built.
Friendship is forgiving, opening your heart.

Friendship is opening your heart.

My Receiving Experience: I have a lot to learn. What people said I repeated in my head. Some people really sent me their message and the person next to me always knew when, because I squeezed their hand real tight!

My Giving Experience: was very good. I could tell by people's expressions that what I was sending them was going straight to their heart. I love to Give. I felt better at giving than I did receiving.

Today we gave thought to what we had learned about peace and peace-makers from these hourly studies with Nobel Prize winners. A great depth of comprehension was reflected in the thoughts of those who are representing these great women and men in the play we are creating called *The Invitation*.

The Invitation is built on a what-if idea – "What if Nobel Peace Prize laureates gathered together in one time and place to discuss peace?" Learning of their lives and reading their thoughts has given us the means to share their experiences. This empathy is bearing fruit in the depth of compassion and passion that we are coming to feel with our heads and think with our hearts. It is an integrating experience that is changing us.

The Invitation touches those who experience it. It does not do justice to what is presented to say that you see it. When you are present, particularly in the Peace Dome, as Mother Teresa, Albert Schweitzer, Martin Luther King, Jr., Linus Pauling, Jimmy Carter, His Holiness the Dalai Lama, Alva Myrdal, and Betty Williams come to life, you see, hear, taste, smell, and feel greatness. What happens in that hour or so, happens both *in* your presence and *because* you are present. It is an amazing experience of being in the world but not of it, of objective and subjective experience occupying the same space. This is why it lingers.

Our first offering of the work in progress was given to over 100 people during a student weekend at the College of Metaphysics on March 30, 2003. At the time, the wet eyes, embracing hugs, and many "thank you's" told the story of people's experiences. Subsequent performances have shown us the potential inherent in the idea.

During one practice I saw a vision of the play performed by others around the world. Actors would vie to portray certain laureates and in the process their lives would be changed. This is using media in a way to uplift, to educate, to inspire, to lead toward peace-filled understanding.

The fact that every six months new students arrive at the College while others depart brought another versatile factor to *The Invitation*. As the people change, so could the laureates involved in the performance. The possible combinations are in the millions making for rich learning for future researchers and scriptwriters.

I could imagine people traveling to the Peace Dome to experience *The Invitation* with the original eight laureates chosen, then returning weeks later to experience a completely different configuration of people. Perhaps in place of Schwietzer and Pauling would be Norman Borlaug and Drs. Bernard Lown and Yevgeny Chazov, founders of International Physicians for the Prevention of a Nuclear War. Jody Williams might speak instead of Betty, Desmond Tutu instead of Mother Teresa. In this way peace would move. It would continually delight. It would breathe.

Anyone who came would experience the wisdom of the laureates, and new revelations could surface in their minds and lives. This had certainly happened for all of us during the development of *The Invitation*. It was like living with Mother Teresa, Martin Luther King, and the others. Increasingly their presence was palpable. They touched our wants and needs, the way we interacted with each other and nature. They made a difference in our lives.

"I have thoughts about Tenzin," said Paul Madar who embodies His Holiness the Dalai Lama. "One of the most significant things I learned was something you pointed out to me at a dinner table conversation we were having. It was about us embodying the laureates. I started talking about how I felt this Dalai Lama consciousness moving through me and all I had to do was receive this Dalai Lama consciousness which is everywhere and there was something you said, 'It's all you. It's all you that you are holding onto. It's *more* of you that you are holding onto.'

"That stuck with me that playing the Dalai Lama was the way that I chose or allowed myself to open up that door to allow the more to come through. That gave me a wide avenue to travel down again and again. It was that part of myself.

"There's a Dalai Lama calendar with his words on each month. This month is about unconditional love and compassion where he defines them succinctly. The essence of compassion is simply wishing the very best for someone and helping them to reach that best."

It was early summer and we had just said goodbye to this year's kids of Camp Niangua, the annual opportunity for children 10-15 to live at the College of Metaphysics. The theme of this year's camp was .... Peace! Campers got to work side by side with the Nobel laureates. They helped create the 9 x 20 foot relief map of the world on the wall supporting the ramp up to the second floor chamber of the Peace Dome.

"After some brain cleansing of my own, I tried to bring that essence of compassion to the Healing Wall work," Paul said. "I wanted the best for the kids. I wanted them to have a really good experience with this. By the end of the week Susie (who at first didn't like the heat or the concrete) couldn't leave without getting her mom and grandma out there to show what she had done. I think they were pretty proud of her, too."

As Paul spoke, my mind projected in the future, twenty years from now. I could put myself in his picture, being a little girl here with Paul, playing in concrete to make a map with him, really having no idea of the depth and breadth of my actions, the impact my actions might have over time and space. Innocence. I could easily imagine what I would grow into in ten, twenty, thirty years. And what I might then think about what I had been a part of – the building of the world's first Peace Dome!

I could feel that thoughtform mushroom inside. Such a gift to our youth is phenomenal to me.

I also remembered when Matthew's parents came to a rehearsal specifically to see their son portray Jimmy Carter. Several weeks later they returned for a performance given family weekend at the College. The human pride in their son was clear. This second time I saw Matthew touch his parents in ways that probably no one else could because he is their son.

Matthew said his mother told him the first time she saw it she was really into it. The second time she appreciated it because she received so many different things from it. "She even asked me if we did it with different lines," Matthew's pride in his mom was evident. "The words spoken are so full I think it is possible to receive something different from it each time."

The spiritual caliber of what we are doing is so potent that I believe Matthew's mother would come every day if it was available.

Laurie Biswell who portrays Betty Williams echoes the multidimensional quality of *The Invitation*. "I received something different each time we presented *The Invitation*. Each week there would be something in it that would grab my attention and be my focus for the next week. What I realized is this is building my own consciousness. I have no idea what Betty Williams is actually like. She is just an idea that I created from her words. She became an idea I could turn on and off. If I was feeling out of sorts I could turn Betty on.

"The most powerful idea Betty expresses is about compassion. There's a line at the beginning of the part of the experience called Discovery where she says, '*Compassion is more important than intellect in calling forth the love that peace needs.*' I look to understand compassion, to know what it is and to bring it out."

I think about this idea about compassion in many ways. One way is brought to me through parenting a child. Dr. Dan (my husband), probably more than Hezekiah (our son) has been a stimulus for me to remain rooted in love. Love, compassion, is a human lesson. I've found that when I am rooted in love everything else takes care of itself. When we are rooted in love, our ability to reason is never a weapon that harms.

I didn't have many preconceived ideas about raising a child, yet doing so has brought Alva-type conflicts between heart and head to the surface. For instance, I was raised in a family where God was at the center, we lived in the truth of loving your neighbor. At the same time – largely because my family's formal education was not beyond high school – I was taught to value education more than spirit. As a result I have found myself constantly challenged to value love first, then learning, with this child. From love comes security, comes goodwill, comes compassion, comes forgiveness, comes all the things that we value as human beings. That focus of concentration called love forms the foundation so the intellect can soar.

Transference of Energy reports, a kind of intuitive diagnosis given through the School of Metaphysics, describe how the individual is using energy. The information highlights what energies you are using and to what purposes, whether that is harmonious to the whole functioning Self or if you are pulling on certain energies to the neglect of others. This is the same thought Betty has.

I think of compassion and intellect as relative to the subconscious mind and the conscious mind, respectively. When you consider thinking with your heart as thinking in subconscious mind you come to realize this involves your understood experiences, your soul. Subconscious mind is where understandings are stored. Many people hear "heart" and they think emotions because their attention is pointed outward away from the soul into the physical world. They have yet to awaken to the world of dreams and the power of intuition. This is where many misconceptions arise between people, between rational men and emotional women. There must be intelligence present for there to be an elevated sense of what the heart is. How to access it, use it, how to make sure it is present in everything.

Betty was trying to get across the idea that we have to stop killing each other. There are big toys that can kill people you don't even know, and those who do so don't even care if a few women or children are cut down. It's called collateral damage. That's cold reason with no compassion or heart.

When we started our journey toward the Peace Dome dedication our goal was simple – prepare ourselves to be living examples of what the *Universal Peace Covenant* says, *"living peaceably begins by thinking peacefully."* With this as our focus we received abundantly.

Erika Scholz, our Mother Teresa, said, "I was thinking about this yesterday when I was in the garden. I was thinking about what it has meant to my consciousness to live in the place where the Peace Dome is coming into being. There is such a powerful thought form that is forming that it is necessary for your consciousness to evolve to meet that peace.

"There is a synchronizing that happens when you live here that is like a necessity. It's like drinking water, because every day you are around the vibration of the Peace Dome. Whatever in you that is not aligned with peace comes out, day after day after day, and you need to — I need to face it and accept and understand and move to higher and higher places of peace. I see so much of my learning has been aligned with removing barriers to peace, inner peace and peace without. I think my experience of playing Mother Teresa was all about that and my lesson that I need to learn was about love.

"Dr. Dan (Condron, her spiritual teacher) has talked to me about love a lot, the importance of it and being able to receive it. That was what Mother Teresa said again and again and again, there needs to be love in the home. I think of that also as there needs to be love in the home, here (pointing to her heart) in order to embrace peace, to understand it, to even hold it in your mind.

"It's been an amazing journey of a whole year in understanding what I need to do to align myself with what is here."

Listening to Erika's words I remembered Mother Teresa's words about the places she would visit and the people would *"have everything, beautiful things she said. Yet everyone is looking at the door."* That is such a human condition. Particularly in the United States we are trained to think of the future, look to the future, everything exists there. This type of thinking, or longing, drags your attention away from the now. In other parts of the world perhaps the emphasis is on the past – tradition, ancester worship, monuments. When Erika spoke of being home, it reminded me of being here now, in the present where past and future meet.

Tad Messenger described his experience of Albert Schweitzer and the Peace Dome as a meeting of the past and future in the now. "It is the energy of the crown chakra. I can see that many, many, many people, their souls and thoughts have gone into this dome from way back from now and in the future. That's what the laureates were like too. Many, many, many people strove for peace, many different times, and that that one thought 'Peace Dome' is focused here which then comes over the campus and over the entire planet. Albert Schweitzer's ruling thought was *reverence for life*. That's what I see it building in me is appreciating more and more the people in my life, and what kind of influence that has for everyone, here, people all over the world who will send in stones (for the Healing Wall) and fabric (for the Peace Tapestries). To be in this area, to be near the dome, to be able to work on the dome, to image and help create this is very great.

"I felt that Albert Schweitzer had a great gratitude for his mission. He struggled a lot and I notice I struggle a lot, too. Yet there is deep reverence in gratitude."

In reflecting upon Jimmy Carter, Matthew said, "Jimmy has been a struggle for me. In the beginning I was all psyched up about portraying him. It was the week after we opened the first floor of the Dome when we read Jimmy's speech at Peacemakers on Sunday. It touched something inside me that I lost pretty quickly. He has this huge utopian vision of peace being achieved through the conscious, purposeful, by choice giving of abundance to others, not where it's communistic – forced by an outside entity – but a generous creation of equality. I held that vision for about a week.

"What started to happen, I was misusing my imagination for a couple months. I started wanting things I didn't have and in doing that I missed what was in my life. I had all these thoughts about Martin Luther King, the Dalai Lama, and Mother Teresa and even the scientists Linus Pauling and Albert Schweitzer. I thought they did outstanding things, and here was Jimmy Carter who I was portraying. In my mind I had all these judgements about him so I missed the power he has. I started to realize that not all of us can be the Dalai Lama, not all of us can be Martin Luther King, Jr., and so forth because we don't have their experiences. But we can all embrace each other as brothers. That's what Jimmy Carter does."

Dr. Dan commented, "The fact is none of us can be another person. That person is a unique individual. It is more a function of whoever we are encountering or learning through or learning with, we have drawn that experience to us so therefore what do we draw from that experience? What do we add to ourselves? Then we build our own understandings. When we add to ourselves, we aid all of humanity.

"That's what all of these people we are talking about have done. They have added enough to their understanding of self that they had a lot to give, moment to moment, day to day, year to year, experience.

"At first you imitate these people like the baby imitates the adult, after a while the imitating graduates to integration not of the person but the lesson into the self. That becomes a part of Self."

Matthew received this saying, "What I learned about Jimmy is that there are two things that he does with his life right now. One is the Carter Foundation where he travels to countries and sets up schools for them. He builds the buildings and brings people in to teach how to sustain themselves, to use their natural environment to live. He doesn't do it all but he is the mobilizer for that. In the States, he is a real activitist for the Habitat for Humanity.

"I see a lot of power in the positions of leadership and it kept me from recognizing the power and influence that is in my own environment. The power and influence that is here is just amazing. What is built here every person on the planet has the ability to build. Everyone has the opportunity to do with their life what Jimmy Carter did with his life.

"I really started to receive the thought that Dr. Barbara gave us when we were discussing the movement of consciousness from Albert in 1952 to Jimmy in 2002. The first speeches in *The Invitation* are from their Nobel acceptance speeches, they move forward in time. The movement we are in as a race is that each of us have the potential to live as Christs, as enlightened beings. Jimmy Carter is a Christian and he has integrity with living his principles. They are his touchstone in making decisions. Everyone has the same opportunity to live his or her principles. The growth is in how and why we interact with each other, and in the way we give."

Christine Madar has a unique point of view of our relationship with the laureates since she is often at the main building greeting visitors and answering the phone while the rest of us rehearse. When I asked her to describe what she had experienced she began with, "I witnessed amazing transformations in the people with each performance. Satyagraha is on my mind a lot.

"I am contributing to a book on psi counseling and I'm writing a chapter on my whole experience with the stillbirth and applying what I've learned in counseling so I have been conjuring up many memories recently. One of the things I was thinking about in the past couple days was that the first time people met to start learning the *Satyagraha* performance given last fall on the College campus was two days before the stillbirth occurred. At that time I was going to be a part of it in the capacity that Erika stepped into as Gandhi's mother and wasn't quite ready for that when the time came, however Dr. Barbara made a place for me in the performance. As a result, that whole experience was special to me becuse of what I experienced at that time. Those living here experienced *Satyagraha,* too, in many different dimensions because the loss affected us all.

"I can remember it was amazing to me how quickly that presentation came together. In three weeks it came together. Then the arc of that with how *The Invitation* subsequently developed and how people transformed even in learning accents. Then the combination of that with the performances by the Niangua campers in the new *Satyagraha.* The part of the opening projection that we do in SOM classes when we envision people from all parts of the world coming together with a common ideal of gaining mastery of consciousness and going forth to bring light into the world, these experiences we have had so far embody that for me in a very real, profound, deep way.

"Shortly after the *Universal Peace Covenant* was written I had an experience where I remember looking at it and I could imagine that this would be a document people would see in many incarnations. Like I imagine that I have read the <u>Bible</u> in, I don't know how many languages, and studied it lifetimes. That's sometimes how I think of the holy works when I think "I've seen these before!" with a different conscious mind and a different setting. It was so clear to me that the Universal Peace Covenant is going to be one of those documents.

"It was thrilling to be conscious at that point of birth. To have that awareness combine with the different experiences we are having. That is what is amazing. There is no carpet in the Dome yet. The mandala will be here in a few months. What it has already been drawing out of us. The Dome demands the best from us. It is like it neutralizes any kind of charge we might have because it demands the best. It doesn't matter if you were Gandhi or Martin Luther King or Mother Teresa walking in here it still demands the same thing of them as all of us sitting here."

Here, in the Peace Dome, all men are created equal.

The Invitation is not really a play, it is an experience. There are something like 150 Nobel Peace Prize laureates, each with their own story and wonderful glimpses of truth and their way of expressing it. Early on I became flexible in my thinking about how to merge these ideas with the document I know these people would appreciate – the *Universal Peace Covenant*.

My flexibility came in response to people and their changeability. There was a time when Matthew wasn't sure if he was going to remain at the College or go to a city, so I made a place for him as a coach rather than as a laureate in the presentation. When he let it be known that he intended to stay past the time of the performance, Jimmy Carter entered *The Invitation*.

Then it struck me that Dr. Pam Blosser needed to be a part of this. I don't know where the thought originated, perhaps from her desire, perhaps from honoring her position as President of the School of Metaphysics, maybe from needing a balance of female-male energy, probably all of them. I looked for someone for her to bring to life and found Alva Myrdal.

From that mobility my mind opened to a greater vision. This was potentially the way to give people the Peace Dome experience. Hearing the thoughts of someone who dedicated their life to peace is stimulating. Hearing the thoughts of eight such people from all backgrounds, occupations, cultures, countries, is mind altering. It grabs people by the hands and pulls them up so they can see from a whole new perspective. Whatever they are willing to look at in themselves – destiny, purpose, need, potential, admittance – they can.

I can imagine the experience changing as the people who live here at the College change thus opening the door for new laureate constellations, new ways of looking at, studying and digesting peace will arise. In time, daily performances will be alive in every sense of the word. From one day to the next the experience will change for those of us giving it and those receiving. One day it can be made of the original eight we started with, on the next day it might be Nelson Mandela, Jody Williams, Norman Bourlaug, Bertha von Suttner, Teddy Roosevelt, Shimon Perez, Rigoberta Menchu, and Aung San Suu Kyi. The combinations of people will be powerful in both their sameness and their difference.

I can imagine that others will hear of this "play" and want to embody these fascinating, thoughtful people, and from doing so their consciousness will grow. This thought can truly change the world. One person at a time.

The Invitation is a good seed born from many lessons learned. Its potential for life is phenomenal because it is bigger than all of us.

A video production of "The Invitation" is available from the School of Metaphysics. See listng of publications at the back of this book.

Jay McCormick

Friendship is —
Loving unconditionally
Listening
Keeping an open mind
giving People the Benefit of the Doubt
Sharing what your thoughts are
Being Honest
Loyal
Being there to share joys & success
Being there to share differences and Pain and help the friend to forgive and learn
Showing and Being sincerely interested in the Person Expecting the best, being hopeful
Kindness

<u>Distill them into one sentence:</u> That conveys image of what friendship is:
A Friend is someone who embodies both Love and truth.

<u>Experience of Receiving</u>
I found that in hearing all of the different perspectives I felt so many different
things . One in particular is: "Friendship is Love with Adventure"

<u>Experience of Giving</u>
I felt that sharing my sentence with so many people —
I did the same thing over and over I got a chance
to hear it more and more.

Paul Madar

<u>My experience of Giving</u>
Everywhere I turned, there were friends.
Friends to the left, Friends to the right, in front of and behind me.
As the circle turned that I was in, I saw a new face — someone I care
about, laugh with, work with, dream with. I bubbled up my one-sentence
definition of friendship on a wave of Love coming out of me. I loved giving it
each time a new face arrived in front of me.

<u>My experience of Receiving</u>
I was so curious to hear what my friends thought about
friendship. The wheel of friendship turned in front of me
and out came love waves with truth. I was drinking in
each person's eyes.

What is friendship?
Charlotte Lafargue Henderson 8-2-2003

Friendship is when I accept someone for who she is.
When I look for ways where there is commonality of thinking.
I look for common interests and share that interest to
strengthen the bond. There I start expanding that sharing
to other areas in order to expand that friendship further.
To see if there are any limits to it.

Friendship is acceptance of who she/he is of what I am.
Respect for that person's differences.
Love of that person just because he is.
Patience to allow the friendship to evolve.
Trust that she will be there for me, that she will be who I think she is.

"Friendship is Acceptance, Respect, Love, Patience, and Trust" given to and received from my friend.

My experience with Giving and Receiving this Friendship Ring

GIVING
At first I was intellectual.
Then I perceived attention and acceptance.
Then I noticed the effects it had on others.
I was moved to a different place in Mind.
I gave of my heart with my words.
I saw how my words, I was received.
I expanded.

RECEIVING
First in my head so I could remember the words and learn
and reflect on them and use them later.
Then I felt moved from brain to heart.
Then I felt and accepted and opened to receive,
to connect with these people, these hearts.
Then I expanded.

SATYAGRAHA

Satya means truth, *graha* means grasping

What is friendship?
John Mestyanek

Responding to the needs of another's soul.
This manifests through love, honesty, communication,
sharing, compassion, connectedness.

My experience was one of great connectedness and love.
I opened my heart to each soul's truth and received
their love fully. It was a wonderful experience of being
comfortable with receiving.

Teresa Starkey

Friendship is nurturing truth in each other.

This is the most profound experience I have ever known in
connection with others. As the receiver, I was so filled
that my need to give could not be contained, and in giving,
I felt the whole connection.

Connecting with people on a deep level, the "real" level,
has been difficult in my life. This has taught me how to be
a receiver, to listen, and then give.

I almost didn't even come this morning,
but "something" told me I needed to be here.
Talina may have been the form of that urging —
now I know why I came.

In the two years since we began to build the Peace Dome, our lives have changed.

I gave increasingly deep thought to each laureate, opening my mind so I could embrace each one like a friend. I wanted intimate knowledge of each and how closer can you get than knowing another's thoughts? That's what reading the Peace Prize laureate's speeches gave me. The concept of communicating the thoughts of peace laureates' to others in this way grew from what they were giving to me each week.

My learning was revealed in the intuitive choices of the people we explored and the order in which they came. Week by week connections were revealed between people's ideas and our current quest to embody peace in the 21st century world. There are several lines of relativity, all revealing Truth that is universal, and how individuals live that Truth.

The first Truth was clear in Mother Teresa's words. She exemplified the part of cosmic consciousness – Christ awareness – that recognizes the human tendency to blame and transforms it into gratitude. When she tells of examining her conscience immediately following the peaceful, thankful death of a woman the sisters had brought into the mission, she faces her own limitations and seeks to clean her own mind and heart.

When seeing how many Western youth are addicted to drugs, she seeks to discover why. Rather than casting blame she identifies the cause as "*there is no one in the family to receive them.*" The parents are busy. They have no time. Younger parents are in some institution, away from the home, so the child wanders without caring direction, and seeking to belong he gets involved with something harmful. The remedy then is love in the home, and where there is love there is gratitude.

There is a Buddhist practice called a gassho. This morning prayer is a powerful medicine for transforming blame into gratitude. The gassho is an attitude accompanied by a particular posture of hands and body and a particular use of breath. The morning gassho is one of gratitude, a recognition of the connectedness of all beings and the appreciation of your part in the whole. I learned this same practice as a Christian child who was taught thank-you prayers with bowed head and hands in the universal prayer pose.

The beauty of gratitude is that it fills your mind with thanksgiving. You realize your abundance and this natural urge to give to others wells up from within you. Thoughts of victimization flee.

What struck me with Martin Luther King was his description of the mind that is willing to take suffering upon itself instead of inflicting it on others. In 2002, those living at the College of Metaphysics brought *Satyagraha* to life. *Satyagraha* is the combination of two Sanskrit words, *satya* meaning truth, and *graha* meaning holding onto, so the concept means "holding onto truth" what M.K. Gandhi called "soul force." Gandhi brought the term to world attention when the nonviolent movement for home rule in India was named for it in the 1940's.

College thespians created a stage presentation that is experiential theater. By unifying the story of Gandhi's life with stories from the Jain tradition, which was the religion of Gandhi's mother, and pairing this with universal principles evidenced in everyone's lives, the reality of one person's enlightened service to a nation becomes real for us all. *Satyagraha* changes people. It lingers long after the physical experience ends.

Satyagraha gives you alternatives where before there seemed to be none.

Even though they never met, Martin Luther King was a student of Gandhi's. Dr. King studied the Indian's thoughts and life. He learned, and what he learned became a cornerstone to the U.S. civil rights movement in the 1960's.

Both King and Gandhi exemplified the ability to overcome resentment with forgiveness. Both men could have built grudges, using the baser instincts of humanity as building blocks for resentment, bitterness, and even hatred. Both men rose above this human weakness to continue giving. When Gandhi was thrown off a train in South Africa he remained in that country for the next seventeen years, giving – again, and again until people of color were acknowledged. In march after march, speech after speech, in the face of inhumanities and imprisonment, King continued giving, again and again.

Forgiveness empowers us to accept and relieve suffering. The action of giving alone is not enough. Many people give with resentment each day, then wonder why others are unpleasant to them or why what they are in a position to receive is drenched in conditions they don't like. Forgiveness means the giver is conscious and aware of his or her purpose in giving. "What is your motive?" forgiveness asks of us.

Martin Luther King, Jr. wanted to change the world. His purpose in giving was very clear, and a nation received his gift accordingly. Replacing resentment with forgiveness is a lesson in peacemaking from Dr. King.

The lesson in Betty Williams' life was striking for me.

When reading of her defining moment filled with the senseless violence that heartlessly snatched life opportunity from three young children, I was there with her. I have known the outrage when others are mistreated, the animal instinct to strike back, the human instinct to protect and defend. I had not described such mental action as revenge until the day we read her words.

It was through seeing how Betty had awakened from her living nightmare, realized the unacceptability of it and determined to make something else happen, that I saw the place revenge plays in keeping conflict going. This came because I could clearly understand how Betty had been willing to see the events happening before her through new eyes. That day on the street, she saw what she had accepted for years differently. The ability to perceive in this way is respect.

When respect is present, the desire to get back at someone, to prove them wrong or us right, to make them feel like we think they made us feel, the satisfaction of besting someone else flees. Respect gives us the ability to be in someone else's shoes, to look through someone else's eyes, to realize our commonalities, and our connection.

Where respect is present, selfishness is seen. We quickly come to realize how we separate ourselves from others. How many people have been ostracized with the thought, "He is not one of us?" How many wars have started because someone, in wanting more, felt they had to take it from someone else? How many times do we think of ourselves first, or solely? How our thoughts and actions affect others determines the quality of our lives.

Albert Schweitzer knew this. His life exemplified the movement from selfishness to selfullness, thus he knew and lived brotherhood with all people whether in the jungles of Africa or the concert halls of Europe. His life proved that living a true humanitarian life brings great riches. I am reminded of an Interfaith sermon I gave years ago, its title was *"When God is your Father, No One is a Stranger."* The wealthiest among us are those who call every man friend.

Abraham Lincoln is one of many who realized the quickest way to defeat your enemy is to make him your friend. Thus sharing our thoughts as well as physical wealth is a means to think differently and live differently. Thinking of what we have to offer others, what might fill their needs, what might be of help to them, centers us in the reality of what the *Universal Peace Covenant* calls *"living peaceably begins by thinking peacefully."* It is the movement from thinking and acting solely for the self to thinking and acting in relationship with others.

To know all people as your brother or your sister is to claim a common ancestry, a common origin. For some, this is recognizing their place in the human race. For others, this is realizing a shared birthright, a mutual destiny. We realize our connectedness with all life. For some, the idea sparks the heart, softening the interaction with love, while others find their head expanding to include others in progressive ways. What is certain is that as the lessons of love are learned we come to understand our humanity.

It was this humanity that led Linus Pauling to question the good judgement of testing nuclear weapons. The evolutionary movement in our species from humankind to reasoners is exemplified in his work. The scientist finds his uniqueness in his ability to use reasoning. Learning how to ask the right questions, opens the door to wisdom. Pauling asked questions about compatibility and relativity resulting in theories of resonance. This is the thrill of people rooting for their team, resonating together when the team scores. It is the beauty of many voices raised in a common prayer.

What Pauling learned, reasoning stimulated him to carry further. "What *are* the effects on the body of radioactive fallout?" he wondered. Could it be humankind was harming itself each time we unleash nuclear particles in the atmosphere? Pauling's search for answers led to conclusions that the pollution of air and water were a major cause of disease as well as mental retardation and physical deformity around the world.

Another question arose, "What can be done to stop this self destruction?" Pauling's answer was to be an activist for the banning of nuclear weapons testing.

I fully believe that it was his exemplary ability to reason that won Pauling Nobel Prize recognition in two fields thus giving him the distinction of being the only person to win Nobels in both a scientific and nonscientific field. The recognition, though perhaps unconscious on the part of those conferring the award, is an awesome example of the heights to which one individual can scale when the head and heart are completely open, functional, and entrained.

Living a harmonious existence is the realm of mystics and masters, and certainly brought into the world through individuals like Tenzin Gyatso. A simple illustration of his enlightened consciousness that I keep in my memory came as the result of a question asked by a reporter. The man asked the Dalai Lama, "When do you think Tibet will be free?"

Tenzin's answer is so clearly lucid, "Tibet will be free when China is free."

"Inner peace is the key: if you have inner peace, the external problems do not affect your deep sense of peace and tranquility. In that state of mind you can deal with situations with calmness and reason, while keeping your inner happiness. That is very important. Without this inner peace, no matter how comfortable your life is materially, you may still be worried, disturbed or unhappy because of circumstances.

"Clearly, it is of great importance, therefore, to understand the interrelationship among these and other phenomena, and to approach and attempt to solve problems in a balanced way that takes these different aspects into consideration."[53]

For me, the Dalai Lama embodies the movement of the reasoner into *intuitive,* Spiritual Man. He is certainly in the world but not of it. As Benjamin Franklin noted during his life, *"My country is the world."* So has His Holiness the 14th Dalai Lama of Tibet made the world his own.

Through these men and women, honored on our planet during the past century, we see the elements that make for peace. By hearing of their lives, we are stimulated in some way. By reading their writings, we align our consciousness with their own, enlightening our thoughts if only for a few hours. By studying their words, we enter their thoughts birthing a respect for them and for ourselves. By living according to the principles they manifested, their work in the world continues through us and in so doing we *"come to know peace in our lifetimes."*

The summer of 2003 brought a new incarnation of the play *Satyagraha*. This rendering actually brought Gandhi to life. Instead of a narrator reading about Gandhi's life, Paul Blosser told his stories and read from Gandhi's "diary" thus revealing the man, his thoughts and his life. I have watched Paul Blosser absorb Gandhi into his being and it is an inspiration to behold. He has such esteem for Gandhi and is devoted to learning from him. Bringing Gandhi to life is natural to him.

Pairing Gandhi with each of the Nobel Peace Laureates was natural for me. There were physical ties to several of them revealed through their own references to Gandhi's influence on their lives. Martin Luther King's life took shape after attending a lecture about Gandhi. H.H. the Dalai Lama speaks of Gandhi as his mentor in his peace prize acceptance speech. The year Gandhi died is the same year Mother Teresa came to India. Seven years later, Alva Myrdal served as ambassador to India from Sweden. I tried to bring these connections to light in how we worked with the interaction between Gandhi's life stories and those of the laureates. What is most telling is how the final movement in the play came into being.

I am so blessed every time I think about the ending of *Satyagraha*. There is a moment when Gandhi is surrounded by the eight Nobel Peace Prize laureates. The connections between them have been revealed one by one and now, standing before you, are nine amazing souls who have walked on this Earth.

How to do justice to them all was the final question to answer, and that answer would form the ending of the play.

Gandhi walks out into history as the narrator describes his passing on the way to a prayer meeting when he was shot in the heart. When he died, Gandhi left a handful of possessions. The image of Gandhi's possessions and others taking them away, one by one, was from the first incarnation of *Satyagraha*. It was poignant and meaningful. I wanted to keep it but had yet to envision how.

When we got to this part in the play, the thespians asked, "In what order will the laureates leave?"

As I had not made time to think it through, I didn't have an answer. I did know that the laureates taking his imaginary possessions would symbolize that they had received from Gandhi though they never met him.

Matthew said, "Let's go in the order we came."

And so we did. I was awestruck. It was Universal Law in action. The movement was absolutely perfect. Tears welled up in my eyes and emotion clenched at my throat as I read the lines and watched the laureates remove Gandhi's treasures.

Jimmy Carter receives Gandhi's tools: two spoons, two pots. Albert Schweitzer inherits Gandhi's three monkeys. Martin Luther King picks up Gandhi's three books: the Gita, the Koran, and the Bible. Tenzin receives the pocket watch, Linus, the eyeglasses, Betty the tin bowl, a souvenir from prison. Alva takes the desk set and Mother Teresa, Gandhi's two pairs of sandals and his khadi. The connections are crystal clear.

In this moment it was as if the hand of God moved upon this play. Each laureate receives from Gandhi something they will find of value in their own life's work. It brings amazing Light every time we perform it.

The lesson from Gandhi's example which keeps revisiting my consciousness can be described as *spirit is all* and *spirit is good.* Gandhi said it so well in describing what satyagraha is. Satya which is truth, comes from the Sanskrit word *sat* meaning "that which is." Gandhi said truth is that which is. Anything else is temporary. The injustice, racial prejudice, hatred, and the like have no existence without our cooperation, meaning we empower such things. We, you and I, bring them into the world. If we want them to go away, we have the power to banish them from our own minds and hearts. This is the place to begin, at home. In the Self.

There is a song composed by my husband called *Amen Om.* The lyrics highlight the essence of man's destiny as described through spiritual scriptures from around the world. The melody is a satisfying blend of feminine and masculine principles. Recently, a line from the song has become my mantra – *"My spirit knows only good."* So simple. So direct. So inviting.

I have found that filling my consciousness with good is sometimes a difficult lesson, for the darkness is tempting. Yet I keep washing my brain of the old ideas of bad and evil. I can at last say I no longer believe in evil, I no longer fear it. I believe and know good.

Clearing the mind of illusion is a powerful medicine. The challenge in life now becomes holding onto truth. I hope in many ways the thoughts shared here help us all to do this.

Satyagraha. May peace be with you all ways.

Friendship —
Barbara Condron

Friendship is God made manifest.
It is love given life. It is what draws the bee to honey,
the butterfly to the flower. It is the fulfillment of our
yearning for wholeness — our desire to be complete.
It is colorblind & tone deaf in a world filled with hues & sounds.
Friendship is the eternal realization that I Am He.

Friendship is God made manifest as I am He.

It is the breath of the Creator expressed through the Universe
as giving & receiving with the fullest of understanding.

Giving — Is living the truth.

Receiving — Is holding onto the truth.

Soul presence. Soul resonance.
Loving the truth — truth between 2 individuals —
bonds already there.
Connectedness in love.

The PeaceMakers

The PeaceMakers in this book are a diverse group of people. They range in age from 8 to 60-something. They are from many ancestries including Africa, German, Irish, English, Mexican, Spanish, French, American Indian. They are professionals and blue collar workers, educated at home, in public and in private schools. They are of many faiths, and none. Here are more details about some of them. Perhaps one of them is like you.

Laurie J. Biswell, 31, is a graduate student at the College of Metaphysics. Previously, she directed the Tulsa School of Metaphysics. Many talented, her work experience ranges from Radio Shack® Sales Associate to Home Health Practitioner to an inspector for Dayton Tire. From her love and vision of the Universal Peace Covenant being displayed in every home, the 2004 Universal Peace Covenant Calendar came to be.

Dr. Pamela Blosser, 56, is from Tulsa, OK. An ordained minister who has earned Doctorates in Metaphysics and Divinity, Dr. Pam holds a degree from Texas Christian University. Currently President of the School of Metaphysics, Pam is also the director of Camp Niangua, a metaphysical camp for young people from ages 10 to 15. A Montessori trained teacher, Dr. Pam believes that teaching children about peace activates a deeper sense of helping other people. She and her husband live in the College of Metaphysics community in Windyville, MO.

Paul Blosser, 49, is currently completing his dissertation for a Doctorate in Metaphysics. He spends half of his time at SOM headquarters, teaching everything from reasoning and astral projection to car maintenance and wood carving, and the other half as a field director for the Chicago area Schools of Metaphysics. It is the way Paul embodies Mohandas K. Gandhi that makes the film "Satyagragha" so real.

Lisa Bold, 35, is single and lives in Dallas, Texas. She has a degree in Criminal Justice. She works for Dr. Pepper as a Sales Representative. Lisa promotes peace by teaching at the Dallas School of Metaphysics.

Gregory Brown, 29, is a College of Metaphysics Graduate Student. He is currently studying the 3rd cycle of lessons. He previously taught at the Kansas City branch of the School of Metaphysics.

Shawn Campbell, 30, is newlywed who works as a nanny and website designer. She is instrumental in the SOM websites (there are three) and directs the Palatine School of Metaphysics. Shawn promotes peace through her work on the School of Metaphysics website www.peacedome.org . She and her husband Adam were married in the Peace Dome just two weeks before its dedication.

Dr. Laurel Clark, 46, is single and lives at the College Of Metaphysics. She has a Bachelor's Degree in Women's Studies from the University Of Missouri. Dr. Laurel serves as a field director for the School of Metaphysics covering the states of Missouri, Indiana & Kentucky. She promotes peace by knowing each individual as a soul. Dr. Laurel stated, "On a soul level all people have common ideals and desires. Everyone comes from the same origin; we are all in this together on planet earth. It is important to help each other grow through living it and teaching it."

Carrie Collins, 27, is the director of the Columbia, MO, School of Metaphysics. She is earning her Doctorate of Metaphysics and works as a landscape artist and horticulturalist. Carrie hosts prayers and meditations nightly and promotes the Universal Hour of Peace and the *Universal Peace Covenant*.

Since 1975, Barbara Condron, 50, has studied and taught the art and science of consciousness through the School of Metaphysics. She practices what she teaches in everything she does, learning daily. She is most pleased this year in her work with the **One Voice** initiative which united people on all seven continents in a synchronized reading of the *Universal Peace Covenant* on the day the Peace Dome was dedicated, October 11, 2003.

Daniel Condron, 50, teaches at the College of Metaphysics where he serves as chancellor. It is largely from his efforts that the Peace Dome was built. He resides at the College of Metaphysics with his wife Barbara and son Hezekiah. He has dedicated his life to enlightenment and aiding others to accomplish the same.

John Crainshaw, 24, is self-employed and lives in Columbia, Missouri where he teaches at the School of Metaphysics. A musician, John creates peace within himself by having a still mind and promotes peace through his paintings and sculptures.

Jonathan Duerbeck, 27 directs the Fayetteville, AR School of Metaphysics. Jonathan has a Bachelor's Degree in Forestry and works as a substitute teacher. He presents public nature programs for children, does lectures and teaches children about peace.

Stacy Ferguson, 23, is a single, dental assistant who directs the Webster Groves (MO) branch of the School of Metaphysics. She practices peace through teaching and being a living example of someone who has created inner peace within herself.

Sharka Glet, 59, was born in the Czech Republic. She left many years ago during an uprising to be free of communism. She came to the US with a degree in art from Charles University in Prague, one small suitcase and her daughter. She lives in Chicago with her husband, works as an artist, and studies and teaches at the School of Metaphysics.

Carol Gunn, 51, is a horticulturalist in Columbia, MO. She promotes peace in sharing what she is learning through her study of Metaphysics.

Mari Hamersley, 50, lives in Newton, Iowa, with her husband and daughter. She has a degree in Spanish and often teaches English as a second language. Mari loves animals and finds peace in helping them find homes through adoption programs. At the School of Metaphysics in Des Moines, IA, Mari teaches meditation as a way of finding inner peace.

John C. Harrison joined the School of Metaphysics in May of 1995. He earned a B.S. in Computer Science from Southeast Missouri State University. John worked as a programmer at Southwestern Bell for 15 years and for EDS for 5 years. He has also held jobs as a carpet cleaner and courier. John is currently a student and teacher at the College of Metaphysics where he is instrumental in creating the data base for the Society for Intuitive Research.

Aaron Krieshok, 24, has traveled the Midwest searching for truth anywhere from studying at the University of Kansas to a spiritual community in the green hills of Northern Wisconsin, from the strings of a guitar to a grass hut in the middle of nowhere Kansas. Now Aaron says he has arrived at the campus of the College of Metaphysics where he is learning that the truth has all along been resting in his own heart waiting to be rediscovered.

Kerry Leigh, 53, is married and has two children, a daughter and a son. Kerry is a landscape architect specializing in ecological restoration. She promotes peace by teaching yoga and meditation.

Christine Madar, 35, devotes time to audio productions and coordinating media for international events such as the annual National Dream Hotline and Universal Hour of Peace from SOM headquarters. She holds a BA in Anthropology and a Doctorate of Divinity. In 1999, she led the first international delegation of metaphysicians to India with the People to People Ambassadors Program. Christine makes a home at the College with her husband Paul where they are devoted to living the principles of the *Universal Peace Covenant*.

Paul Madar is 38, married, and currently lives at the Headquarters of the School of Metaphysics where he will raise his new child in a metaphysical community. He has a B.S. in Biology, a Masters in Business and extensive studies in music. As a graduate teacher, he helps produce educational and inspirational audio and video projects of music, lectures, workshops about how to create peace within. Paul strives to embody the qualities of the Dalai Lama in compassion, insight, and universal responsibility.

Matthew Marian, 25, is from St. Louis Mo. He is a teacher at the Louisville, KY, SOM. He promotes peace through thoughts and prayers and reading the *Universal Peace Covenant* every day. Matthew knows that peace has to start within each individual and then can move to others, spreading like a ripple affecting more and more people gaining momentum and creating a wave of peace.

Tad W. Messenger has been a student at the School of Metaphysics from 1984-1989, and from 1997 to the present time. He is a student-teacher at the College of Metaphysics since 2000. He earned a B.A. with a major in religion from the College of Wooster, a B.S. in geology from S.U.N.Y. Brockport and completed the Masters program in Geology at M.U. at Columbia. His life long goal is to build the College of Metaphysics.

John Mestyanek, 23, is director for the SOM in Urbana, IL. He is well traveled and has lived all over the US. He works as a teacher's aid for special needs children, grades 1-5. John has planted a Peace Pole and holds a Circle of Love every week offering prayers and meditation for peace.

Nancy Mitter is a Dental Hygienist living in Columbia, MO. She is married and has three children. She promotes peace through giving and sharing what she is learning in creating her own inner peace.

Teresa Padilla, 42, is married with one daughter. She holds an associate degree in marketing, broadcasting and classic piano, and a Doctorate in Divinity. Teresa has dual residence, one in Southern MO and another in Kansas City, KS. She is a field director for SOM promoting peace through teaching teachers to live by example and to teach their students about peace, thus planting the seeds of peace and spreading peace throughout the world.

Dave Rosemann, arrived as a College of Metaphysics student in July of 2003. Previously, he was a teacher in the Columbia and Springfield, Missouri School of Metaphysics branches. He is 24 years old. He has a Bachelors of Science in Mass Media, minoring in Religious Studies from Southwest Missouri State University. He has worked in the fields of live sound production, audio recording, and music promotion. Dave has Cerebral Palsy and is using what he is learning in his studies with visualization and concentration to cause permanent healing within his body.

With an undergraduate degree in communication and a Master of Science in Education, Erika Scholz has always had a strong desire to work with people in a way that could inspire and uplift. As an elementary English as a Second Language teacher, she had an opportunity to do just that, aiding others to abundance as she successfully employed metaphysical principles in her classroom. She has directed a SOM in Dallas, studied for a little over a year at the College of Metaphysics, and is now in opening a branch of SOM in Milwaukee. Erika is currently working towards earning her Doctorate of Divinity and aspires to become a Psi Counselor through the School of Metaphysics.

Chris Sheehan, 23, married, and is studying in the second cycle of lessons at SOM World Headquarters in Windyville, Missouri. With an Associates of Applied Arts degree in Graphic Design and over 10 years experience in the realm of artistic expression, he loves being a part of the continual creation of consciousness reflected in the beauty of our campus. Previousy a teacher and director of the Dallas branch of the School of Metaphysics he has come to the College of Metaphysics to learn about service.

Bibliography

Where to find more.
http://www.nobel.se/nobel/nobel-foundation/publications/lectures/index.html

Nobel Peace Prize Laureates featured in this book include:

2002
Jimmy Carter USA 39th President of the United States of America b. 1924-

1989
The 14th Dalai Lama (Tenzin Gyatso) Tibet   b. 1935-

1982
Alva Myrdal (shared prize) Sweden, former Cabinet Minister; Diplomat; Writer
b. 1902 - d. 1986

1979
Mother Teresa   India   Leader of Missionaries of Charity, Calcutta b. 1910 (in
Skoplje, then Turkey) - d. 1997

1976
Betty Williams and Mairead Corrigan   United Kingdom
Founders of the Northern Ireland Peace Movement (later renamed Community of Peace
People) b. 1943 -

1964
Martin Luther King Jr.   USA   Leader of "Southern Christian Leadership Conference"
b. 1929 - d. 1968

1962
Linus Carl Pauling USA   California Institute of Technology   Pasadena, CA, USA
b. 1901 - d. 1994

1952
Albert Schweitzer
France
Missionary surgeon; Founder of Lambaréné (République de Gabon)
b. 1875 (in Kaysersberg, then Germany)   d. 1965

The Nobel Peace Prize 1901
Jean Henri Dunant (shared prize) Switzerland
Founder of the International Committee of the Red Cross, Geneva; Originator Geneva
Convention (Convention de Genève)
Founder and President of first French peace society (since 1889 called Société française
pour l'arbitrage entre nations)
b. 1828 - d. 1910

Additional titles available from SOM Publishing include:

The Tao Te Ching: Interpreted and Explained
Dr. Daniel Condron   ISBN 0944386-30-x $15.00

Atlantis: The History of the World Vol. 1
Drs. Daniel & Barbara Condron   ISBN 0944386-28-8 $15.00

How to Raise an Indigo Child
Dr. Barbara Condron ISBN 0944386-29-6 $14.00

Interpreting Dreams for Self Discovery
Dr. Laurel Clark & Paul Blosser ISBN 0944386-25-3 $12.00

Karmic Healing
Dr. Laurel Clark ISBN 0944386-26-1 $15.00

The Bible Interpreted in Dream Symbols
Drs. Condron, Condron, Matthes, Rothermel
ISBN 0944386-23-7 $18.00

Spiritual Renaissance
Elevating Your Conciousness for the Common Good
Dr. Barbara Condron   ISBN 0944386-22-9 $15.00

Superconscious Meditation
Kundalini & the Understanding of the Whole Mind
Dr. Daniel R. Condron   ISBN 0944386-21-0 $13.00

First Opinion: Wholistic Health Care in the 21st Century
Dr. Barbara Condron   ISBN 0944386-18-0 $15.00

The Dreamer's Dictionary
Dr. Barbara Condron ISBN 0944386-16-4 $15.00

The Work of the Soul
Dr. Barbara Condron, ed. ISBN 0944386-17-2 $13.00

Uncommon Knowledge Past Life & Health Readings
Dr. Barbara Condron, ed. ISBN 0944386-19-9 $13.00

The Universal Language of Mind
The Book of Matthew Interpreted
Dr. Daniel R. Condron ISBN 0944386-15-6 $13.00

Permanent Healing
Dr. Daniel R. Condron ISBN 0944386-12-1 $9.95

Dreams of the Soul - The Yogi Sutras of Patanjali
Dr. Daniel R. Condron ISBN 0944386-11-3 $13.00

Kundalini Rising
Mastering Your Creative Energies
Dr. Barbara Condron ISBN 0944386-13-X $13.00

To order write:

School of Metaphysics
World Headquarters
163 Moon Valley Road
Windyville, Missouri 65783   U.S.A.

Enclose a check or money order payable in U.S. funds to SOM with any order.
Please include $4.00 for postage and handling of books, $8 for international
orders.

A complete catalogue of all book titles, audio lectures and courses, and videos is
available upon request.

Visit us on the Internet at *http://www.som.org*
e-mail: som@som.org

The Invitation
the hour and twenty minute presentation written about in this book
is available on video and DVD from the School of Metaphysics.

MakingPeace
a twenty minute film about the building of the Peace Dome from
the Spring of 2001 to a few days before its dedication October 11,
2003 is available on video and DVD from the School of Metaphysics.

Satyagraha
the presentation centered on Mohandas K. Gandhi's life and his
indelible imprint upon eight Nobel Peace Laureates is in production
with an anticipated release date in early 2004.

The Story of *Paz & Shanti*
is being illustrated by Chris and Simone Sheehan and will be published in 2004.

We are seeking benefactors to make these works widely available
around the world. One hundred percent of the proceeds of these
productions go toward the Peace Dome. If you support the Peace
Dome and what it represents let us hear from you.

The Peace Dome was dedicated as a universal site for Peace on October 11, 2003.

Over a dozen mayors from Honolulu to Denver to Miami, the governors of Tennessee and Iowa, and President Rauf Dentkas of Northern Cypress proclaimed a "Moment of Peace" in their lands in honor of this history-making event. People on all seven continents, including two at the South Pole, joined as One Voice in the first worldwide simultaneous reading of the *Universal Peace Covenant*. Their amazing stories are told at www.peacedome.org

The *Covenant* is now read at the turn of each new year, December 3lst into January 1st. In this way one of the lines from the covenant comes alive as we cause *"peace to move across the face of the earth."* Please join us, wherever you are, so we *"might know the power of peace in our lifetimes."*

May peace be with you all ways.

We invite you to become a special part of our efforts to aid in enhancing and quickening the process of spiritual growth and mental evolution of the people of the world. The School of Metaphysics, a not-for-profit educational and service organization, has been in existence for three decades. During that time, we have taught tens of thousands directly through our course of study in applied metaphysics. We have elevated the awareness of millions through the many services we offer. If you would like to pursue the study of mind and the transformation of Self to a higher level of being and consciousness, you are invited to write to us at the School of Metaphysics World Headquarters in Windyville, Missouri 65783.

*The heart of the School of Metaphysic*s is a four-tiered course of study in understanding the mind in order to know the Self. Lessons introduce you to the Universal Laws and Truths which guide spiritual and physical evolution. Consciousness is explored and developed through mental and spiritual disciplines which enhance your physical life and enrich your soul progression. For every concept there is a means to employ it through developing your own potential. Level One includes concentration, visualization (focused imagery), meditation, and control of life force and creative energies, all foundations for exploring the multidimensional Self.

*As experts in the Universal Language of Min*d, we teach how to remember and understand the inner communication received through dreams. We are the sponsors of the National Dream Hotline®, an annual educational service offered the last weekend in April. Study centers are located throughout the Midwestern United States. If there is not a center near you, you can receive the first series of lessons through correspondence with a teacher at our headquarters.

For those desiring spiritual renewal, weekends at our Moon Valley Ranch on the College of Metaphysics campus in the Midwest U.S. offer calmness and clarity. Full Spectrum™ training is given during these Spiritual Focus Weekends. Each weekend focuses on intuitive research done specifically for you in your presence. More than a traditional class or seminar, these gatherings are experiences in multidimensional awareness of who you are, why you are here, where you came from, and where you are going.

The Universal Hour of Peace was initiated by the School of Metaphysics on October 24, 1995 in conjunction with the 50th anniversary of the United Nations. We believe that peace on earth is an idea whose time has come. To realize this dream, we invite you to join with others throughout the world by dedicating your thoughts and actions to peace for one hour beginning at 11:30 p.m. December 31st into the first day of January each year. Help us cause *"peace to move across the face of the earth"* by reading the Universal Peace Covenant at the turning of the new year. Living peaceably begins by thinking peacefully. Please contact us about how you can become a Peace Correspondent.

There is the opportunity to aid in the growth and fulfillment of our work. Donations supporting the expansion of the School of Metaphysics' efforts are a valuable way for you to aid humanity. As a not-for-profit publishing house, SOM Publishing is dedicated to the continuing publication of research findings that promote peace, understanding and good will for all of Mankind. It is dependent upon the kindness and generosity of sponsors to do so. Authors donate their work and receive no royalties. We have many excellent manuscripts awaiting a benefactor.

One hundred percent of the donations made to the School of Metaphysics are used to expand our services. The world's first Peace Dome located on our college campus was funded entirely by individual contributions. Presently, donations are being received for the Octadome an international center for multidimensional living. Donations to the School of Metaphysics are tax-exempt under 501(c)(3) of the Internal Revenue Code. We appreciate your generosity. With the help of people like you, our dream of a place where anyone desiring Self awareness can receive education in mastering the mind, consciousness, and the Self will become a reality.

We send you our Circle of Love.